GLOBAL AGRICULTURE *and the* AMERICAN FARMER

GLOBAL AGRICULTURE

and the

AMERICAN FARMER

OPPORTUNITIES FOR
U.S. LEADERSHIP

KIMBERLY ANN ELLIOTT

CENTER FOR GLOBAL DEVELOPMENT
Washington, D.C.

Library of Congress Cataloging-in-Publication data
Names: Elliott, Kimberly Ann, 1960– author.
Title: Global agriculture and the American farmer : opportunities for U.S. leadership / by Kimberly Ann Elliott.
Description: Washington, D.C. : Center For Global Development, [2017] | Includes bibliographical references and index.
Identifiers: LCCN 2016057406 | ISBN 9781933286983 (pbk.)
Subjects: LCSH: Agriculture and state—United States. | Agriculture and state—Developing countries.
Classification: LCC HD1761 .E452 2017 | DDC 338.1/873—dc23 LC record available at https://lccn.loc.gov/2016057406

987654321

Composition by Elliott Beard

CONTENTS

PREFACE

AMERICAN FARMERS ARE AMONG THE most productive in the world and the United States is one of the world's largest producers and exporters of a range of staple foods. The U.S. government is also, by far, the largest provider of bilateral aid for agriculture in developing countries. American policies will thus have disproportionate effects on whether the world achieves the Sustainable Development Goals of ending the hunger and extreme poverty still found in many rural areas. U.S. policies also affect the provision of global public goods that are important for development.

The problem addressed in this book is that some U.S. policies to support domestic farmers conflict with efforts to use agriculture as an antipoverty tool abroad. The United States is not alone in subsidizing agriculture, and it is by no means the worst offender in this regard. But its outsized role in agricultural markets makes American leadership the key to progress in this area. In this book Senior Fellow Kimberly Elliott focuses on three areas where U.S. policies disproportionately favor farm interests *and* do so in ways that are particularly damaging for the poor and vulnerable in developing countries: agricultural subsidies and trade barriers that distort global markets; biofuel mandates that fail to mitigate climate change; and the failure to adequately regulate antibiotic use in livestock, which contributes to the global spread of antibiotic-resistant "super bugs."

U.S. agricultural subsidies impose costs on U.S. taxpayers. And, by pushing down global food prices, they make it harder for poor farmers and rural workers in developing countries to earn a decent living in agriculture.

In the mid-2000s U.S. (and European Union) policymakers ratcheted up policies to promote the use of food-based biofuels as a means of reducing dependence on oil imports and reducing greenhouse gas emissions from fossil fuels. However, these policies raise the risk of additional deforestation or other land use changes to replace the food crops now going into fuel tanks. These negative effects on forests and soil quality, among other things, could mean that the net impact of this generation of biofuels is more carbon in the atmosphere, not less.

Finally, effective antibiotics are another global public good put at risk by certain agricultural policies. Until recently, U.S. regulators allowed farmers and ranchers to buy antibiotics over the counter—mixed in feed or in water-soluble form—to promote growth in healthy animals, rather than solely to treat sick ones. Without further steps, livestock producers could still use large amounts of antibiotics in similar ways to prevent disease in large-scale animal feeding operations. These uses encourage the survival of drug-resistant bacteria, increasing the risk of deadly antibiotic-resistant infections in people. The threat is particularly potent in developing countries where clean water and sanitation are insufficient and the disease burden is high. The modest steps that U.S. and other policymakers have taken to reduce antibiotic use in livestock do not go nearly far enough. Moreover, the response must be global to be fully effective.

While noting that broad, often global, reforms are needed to fix each of these problems, Elliott identifies practical steps that U.S. policymakers could take in the relatively short run to improve farm policies for American taxpayers and consumers as well as for the poor and vulnerable in developing countries. With this volume Elliott builds on the analysis in her previous CGD book, _Delivering on Doha: Farm Trade and the Poor_ (copublished with the Peterson Institute for International Economics). _Global Agriculture and the American Farmer_ adds to a body of CGD work examining how aid, trade, and other policies in the advanced countries can do a better job in addressing food security and rural poverty in developing countries. We hope that this volume contributes to the debate over needed reforms by distilling any number of complex and sometimes hard-to-follow U.S. policies into an accessible form.

Masood Ahmed

PRESIDENT

CENTER FOR GLOBAL DEVELOPMENT

ACKNOWLEDGMENTS

THIS BOOK HAS BEEN A long time in the making, and first and foremost I would like to thank Nancy Birdsall for her strong encouragement throughout. As with my previous book on agriculture, *Delivering on Doha*, David Orden was an indispensable resource, and I am extremely grateful for his continued help and support. Joe Glauber also read more than one draft and allowed me to plumb his deep knowledge on farm bill and agricultural trade issues. I am grateful to CGD colleagues Alan Gelb and Erin Collinson for reading the entire manuscript and providing their usual clear-headed and insightful comments. I also benefited greatly from the comments of an anonymous reviewer and the discussion in a January 2016 study group, including (in addition to those named above) Grace Burton, Charles Kenny, Gawain Kripke, Will Martin, John Osterman, Erik Pederson, Vijaya Ramachandran, and Emmy Simmons. While any remaining errors are mine alone, they surely would be more numerous without the help I received from so many generous and patient colleagues.

Last but by no means least, the book would not have been possible without the research assistance of Ted Collins and Albert Alwang. Janeen

Madan was the last of this excellent group and did yeoman's work assisting with the final research tasks, as well as in pulling everything together. I would also like to thank Rajesh Mirchandani, Emily Schabacker, and the rest of the CGD communications team for their help in producing and promoting this book.

1

AGRICULTURE, DEVELOPMENT, AND GLOBAL PUBLIC GOODS

U.S. Policies at Cross Purposes

THE CENTRAL AIMS OF THE Sustainable Development Goals are to eliminate extreme poverty and hunger by 2030. As the goals recognize, this will not happen without attention to agriculture. Right now, a billion people scrape by on just over $1 per day. Most of them live in rural areas and most are dependent on agriculture for their meager livelihoods. On any given day, millions more are at risk of falling back into poverty because of a bad harvest or an unexpected illness. Even though they farm for a living, these families are often malnourished and hungry. An estimated 150 million children younger than age five will have their growth stunted by malnutrition, and many will suffer life-long health and cognitive problems as a result. The global poor are also most at risk from climate change, which has obvious links to agriculture, and are vulnerable to antibiotic-resistant diseases, which have less-well-understood connections to agricultural practices.

The United States is one of the world's largest producers and exporters of a range of agricultural commodities, so U.S. policies that affect agriculture will play a large role in whether the international community can end hunger and extreme poverty, and do so sustainably. During the food price spikes of 2007–08, President George W. Bush sharply increased foreign assistance for food security and nutrition. His successor, Barack Obama, with strong support from Congress, created Feed the Future and the New Alliance for Food Security and Nutrition to provide assistance for (climate-smart) agricultural development in food-insecure countries.

Yet U.S. policies often work at cross purposes. Since before World War II, the United States has provided subsidies and trade protection to farmers in ways that suppressed global prices on global markets, distorted incentives to invest in developing country agriculture, and undermined the livelihoods of poor farmers in other countries. Then, just as the long-run secular decline in agricultural prices seemed to be bottoming out, the United States and the European Union (EU) ratcheted up policies promoting demand for food-based biofuels, which helped turn modestly rising food prices into sharp spikes that roiled global markets. And when commodity prices started falling again in 2013–14, the U.S. Congress ensured that subsidy programs were in place to shield American farmers from revenue declines.

In addition to the price and other global market distortions from U.S. (and other) farm programs, some agricultural policies create negative global spillovers because of what they fail to do. Biofuel support policies were touted as part of the solution to climate change, but both U.S. and European policymakers failed to develop effective sustainability criteria to ensure that would be the case. Instead, corn-based ethanol and oilseed-based biodiesel may well be increasing greenhouse gas (GHG) emissions, relative to their fossil fuel counterparts. Another growing concern is the use of massive amounts of antibiotics to promote growth and prevent disease in livestock, which contributes to the proliferation of antibiotic-resistant bacteria. Despite long-standing concerns, U.S. authorities have only recently taken modest steps to regulate the practice.

American policymakers are genuinely committed to promoting global food security and poverty alleviation, addressing climate change, and combating antimicrobial resistance. And farmers face risks that markets cannot handle, so there is a role for public policy. But policymakers all too often fail to ensure that the agriculture sector shoulders a fair share of the burden of the negative spillovers that it produces. This book focuses on

U.S. agricultural policies and practices in these three areas—traditional agricultural subsidies, biofuels, and the use of antibiotics in livestock—because they have global implications that are particularly harmful for the poor and food-insecure in developing countries. Of course, American consumers and taxpayers would also benefit from such reforms.

THE AGRICULTURE AND DEVELOPMENT DEBATE SHIFTS

In the first decade of the new millennium, the goals of reducing poverty and hunger sometimes seemed to be in conflict. When food prices spiked in 2007–08, some experts estimated that more than 100 million people might fall into deeper poverty and go hungry. Many blamed biofuel subsidies and mandates in rich countries for diverting food crops for fuel. Just a few years before, however, agricultural prices had been at historically low levels and the debate around rural poverty was starkly different. At that time, high-income countries were in the spotlight because they were providing billions of dollars in support to their relatively well-off producers at the expense of millions of poor farmers in developing countries.[1]

In the wake of the food price spikes, advanced country governments responded with rather more alacrity than they had to the earlier criticisms of their price-suppressing policies. But they did so in a limited way. In L'Aquila, Italy, in 2009, the Group of 8 (G8) industrialized countries put food insecurity at the top of the development agenda and committed $20 billion over three years to address it. President Barack Obama launched the Feed the Future initiative in 2010 and pledged $3.5 billion for the effort. In 2014, the administration's ongoing commitment included spending a total of $2.4 billion for Feed the Future and "related food security funding," including nonemergency food aid.[2]

What is striking, however, is what the United States and other G8 countries did not do. They have mostly not reformed policies that undermine food security and generate negative global spillovers if it would mean taking on their own domestic agricultural interests. To the contrary, both the United States and the EU ramped up their support for bio-

1. Elliott (2006).
2. Feed the Future (2015, p. 75).

fuels in 2008–09 (though the EU later backtracked a bit). In 2008, and again in 2014, the U.S. Congress passed farm bills that maintained an array of subsidies for American farmers. Overall, from 2002 to 2013 the U.S. government spent not quite $10 billion for agriculture and nutrition assistance to developing countries and more than $300 billion to support the incomes of American farmers.[3]

The United States is not the world's worst offender when it comes to supporting the agriculture sector. The levels of trade-distorting farm support remain far higher in Japan, Korea, and much of Europe. But the United States is among the world's largest producers and exporters of a number of agricultural commodities, and Congress has shown a great reluctance to stop intervening in agricultural markets.[4] The United States is also the world's largest market for biofuels and one of the largest users of antibiotics in livestock. While pressures are growing for reform in all three areas, the forces opposing it are potent.

Although the EU still provides billions of dollars in overall agricultural support, it has gone further in addressing concerns about its agricultural policies. EU policymakers converted most producer support to less trade-distorting forms and reduced the incentives to consume more food-based biofuels. They responded to the antimicrobial resistance threat with more vigorous action against antibiotic use in livestock than in the United States to date. Each chapter thus draws contrasts with EU policy as applicable.

The policies of large emerging markets where beggar-thy-neighbor policies are beginning to take root are also of increasing interest. In addition to providing potentially trade-distorting support to farmers, India's decision to ban wheat and rice exports in 2007 contributed to the price spikes for those commodities. While China's support for farmers is expanding, alarm over the use of antibiotics in its industrializing livestock sector is increasingly urgent. Thus another reason it is important for the United States to reform is that emerging powers are not likely to respond to "do as I say, not as I do" rhetoric.

---

3. Data are from the Organization for Economic Cooperation and Development's Creditor Reporting System and Producer Support Estimates databases.
4. Elliott (2006, chap. 3).

PLAN OF THE BOOK

Chapter 2 begins by providing background on the important role of agriculture in many of the world's poorest countries and how the shifts in agricultural markets in the 2000s affected them. Agriculture is the largest source of employment in the poorer countries and is also often an important source of export revenues. But food also accounts for a large share of household expenditures for the poor, and many poor farmers are net buyers of food because of their low productivity. Thus, higher food prices can increase poverty in the short run where the number of poor net buyers exceeds the number of poor net sellers. A growing body of research suggests, however, that (somewhat) higher prices reduce poverty in the medium and long run.

Chapter 3 turns to the problems presented by agricultural subsidies and trade barriers. Government support for agriculture has declined in most high-income countries since the 1990s. However, this decline in support occurred mostly because rising prices reduced the need for subsidies, and only in a few cases because governments embraced policy reform. The U.S. Congress passed a farm bill in 2014 that took some steps in a more market-oriented direction, but it did so in ways that put U.S. programs at odds with the direction of reform embodied in international trade rules. And because the policy reforms in the United States and other high-income countries remain incomplete at best, the distorting impact of subsidies and trade barriers will resurface if commodity prices resume their earlier trend decline.

Chapter 4 turns to biofuel policies. The United States and the EU boosted support for biofuel consumption at a time when commodity markets were already tightening, and they did so mostly through inflexible mandates, which contributed importantly to the food price spikes in 2007–08. The price volatility created by these policies had negative consequences for consumers and producers alike. Worse, there is growing research showing that food-based biofuels are increasing GHG emissions, not reducing them as claimed.

Finally, chapter 5 explores how the failure to adequately regulate livestock production is an indirect subsidy that contributes to the production of negative externalities. Many of these "public bads" are local in nature—for example, air or water pollution arising from poor manure management or pesticide runoff. But the focus in chapter 5 is the problem of increasingly nasty bacteria that do not respond to antibiotics and do not respect borders. The link to agriculture comes from the fact that more antibiotics are used in livestock than in people every year, and many producers use them to promote faster growth in their animals and prevent disease in the large, confined feeding operations that are increasingly common around the world.

Chapter 6 wraps up by summarizing general lessons that emerge from the policy failures analyzed in the three core chapters, including vulnerability to policy capture by concentrated interests and the need for flexibility when the information available to policymakers is incomplete or imperfect. The chapter also summarizes priorities for U.S. reforms in each area, including the following efforts:

- Reduce the amount of the subsidy that farmers receive for buying crop insurance (now more than 60 percent of the value of the average premium).

- Reform the complicated and increasingly expensive program protecting domestic sugar producers and remove the tight restrictions on imports.

- Remove the requirements to purchase food aid in the United States and transport it long distances on U.S.-flagged ships.

- Eliminate the current mandate to blend biofuels in gasoline and diesel, or at least make the mandate more flexible and reduce the amount of biofuel that is derived from food crops.

- Agree to global targets to reduce the use of antibiotics in livestock and ensure that veterinarians who oversee such use do not have financial incentives to prescribe antibiotics.

The chapter notes that the push for reforms has to begin with U.S. taxpayers, consumers, and other stakeholders who directly pay for these policies. But, with respect to agricultural subsidies, global cooperation would help to overcome international collective action problems that could otherwise block reform. And when it comes to combating antibiotic resistance, success simply is not possible without global cooperation.

In sum, U.S. policies that aim to reduce rural poverty, promote food security, mitigate climate change, and improve health outcomes in developing countries are all too often at odds with policies supporting a small number of American farmers. This policy incoherence raises the costs of achieving each of these important goals, and it undermines U.S. leadership when it is desperately needed.

2

AGRICULTURE, POVERTY, AND FOOD
SECURITY IN POOR COUNTRIES

AGRICULTURE IS A KEY SECTOR for poverty alleviation and food security in developing countries. The world's poorest people mostly live in rural areas and depend on agriculture (directly or indirectly) for income. Yet rapidly rising prices can also be a problem for the rural poor in the short run because many of them have to buy food to supplement their meager harvests. The roller coaster ride that commodity prices have been on since the mid-2000s has not been helpful in finding sustainable solutions to these problems. Chapter 3 will examine how the agricultural policies in high-income countries contributed to the early price slumps, while chapter 4 will delve into the role of biofuels in the later price spikes. Before turning to those stories, however, it is useful to briefly review what has happened overall in agricultural markets since the dawn of the new millennium and how these changes have affected developing countries.

SHIFTING GLOBAL MARKETS FOR AGRICULTURE

As a result of scientific and management innovations, productivity improved and real agricultural commodity prices generally declined over the 20th century, despite rapid population and economic growth. In the

Figure 2-1   Annual Real Food Price Index, 1960–2015

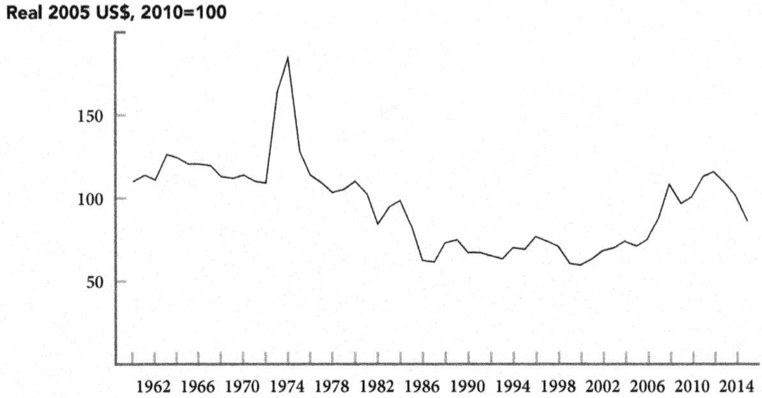

Real 2005 US\$, 2010=100

Source: World Bank Commodity Price Data (accessed October 2016).

first decade of the 2000s, the declining trend in prices seemed to have halted, at least temporarily, as yield gains slowed and demand in developing countries grew (figure 2-1). Food prices were just beginning to recover from the lows of the late 1990s when a confluence of factors led to a sharp spike in 2007–08. A second spike followed in 2010–11 before food prices began falling in the latter half of 2013. In 2015, however, real food prices were still more than 40 percent higher than the trough in 1999–2000, and monthly prices showed a modest recovery in 2016.

A range of cyclical and structural factors, as well as policies, played a role in the price swings that marked the first decade of the new millennium.[1] Setting the stage was the decision by China to draw down the large grain stocks that it had accumulated at the end of the 1990s (figure 2-2). Global stocks of corn, rice, and wheat fell from a peak of nearly 550 million metric tons in the late 1990s to a bit over 300 million metric tons a few years later. The level of stocks relative to demand for corn, wheat, and rice fell from 25–30 percent in the 1990s to just over 15 percent in 2006–08.[2]

Unusually low grain stocks meant that there was very little cushion to

1. The United Nations Food and Agriculture Organization (FAO 2009, pp. 15–22) provides a summary of the extensive literature on causes of the 2007–08 price shocks.

2. See Schnepf (2008, p. 6) and Abbott, Hurt, and Tyner (2008, p. 12). The U.S. Department of Agriculture's Production, Supply, and Distribution database reports the global stocks-to-use ratio for various commodities.

Figure 2-2 Global Stocks of Corn, Rice, and Wheat, 1995–2009

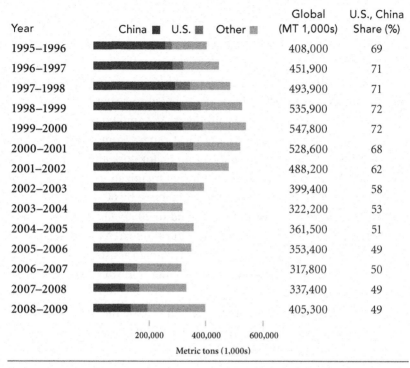

Year	China ▪ U.S. ▪ Other ▪	Global (MT 1,000s)	U.S., China Share (%)
1995–1996		408,000	69
1996–1997		451,900	71
1997–1998		493,900	71
1998–1999		535,900	72
1999–2000		547,800	72
2000–2001		528,600	68
2001–2002		488,200	62
2002–2003		399,400	58
2003–2004		322,200	53
2004–2005		361,500	51
2005–2006		353,400	49
2006–2007		317,800	50
2007–2008		337,400	49
2008–2009		405,300	49

200,000 400,000 600,000
Metric tons (1,000s)

Source: U.S. Department of Agriculture's Production, Supply, and Distribution database (accessed May 2016).

absorb sudden changes in demand, such as for biofuels under new government mandates in the United States and the EU. Prolonged drought in Australia added an unusually severe supply-side shock in wheat markets. The shocks in agricultural markets were further exacerbated by macroeconomic trends outside agriculture. The declining dollar contributed by dampening price increases in foreign currency terms, which increased demand for U.S. exports and further boosted the U.S. dollar price. Investors and speculators also increasingly turned to commodity futures markets to hedge their risks, first from inflationary expectations and then from the popping of the real estate bubble.[3] As discussed in more detail in

3. Trostle (2008).

chapter 4, sharply rising energy prices both further increased the demand for alternative fuels, including crop-based biofuels, and raised agricultural production costs. For example, fertilizer, which is energy-intensive to produce, was two to four times more expensive in May 2008 than it had been in 2006.

Underlying these cyclical factors, rapid income growth in large developing countries, especially China, contributed to rising food consumption, especially of meat and dairy products. The amount of grain or other feed required to produce a pound of meat ranges from nearly 3 pounds for poultry to as much as 7 pounds, or more, for pork and beef.[4] Overall, the United Nations Food and Agriculture Organization (FAO) has projected that food production will have to increase by 60 percent from the mid-2000s level to meet increased demand in 2050.[5] On the supply side, advanced country investments in agricultural research and development were slowing, even as yield growth slowed. Foreign assistance and government investments in agriculture in developing countries also fell sharply in the 1980s and 1990s.

It is possible that commodity prices will resume the downward trend they were on for much of the 20th century. But there are also reasons to think that prices will remain firmer for some time.[6] Population and income growth will continue to put upward pressure on demand and prices unless there are adequate investments to boost productivity and ensure that supply keeps up.[7] Climate change adds to the longer-run challenge of producing enough food and is likely to exacerbate short-run volatility, especially in sub-Saharan Africa, as extreme weather events become more frequent.[8]

4. Trostle (2008, p. 12).
5. FAO (2012b).
6. OECD-FAO (2015, p. 49).
7. FAO (2009, pp. 4–5).
8. Cline (2007).

THE AGRICULTURE SECTOR IN POOR COUNTRIES

About half the population in developing countries still lives in rural areas. Most depend on agriculture for their livelihoods.[9] In the lowest-income countries, agriculture accounts for three-quarters of employment and a third of GDP. All too many of those working in agriculture are subsistence farmers or landless laborers who barely eke out a living for their families. According to International Fund for Agricultural Development (IFAD) estimates for the late 2000s, rural areas were home to roughly 1 billion people living in extreme poverty (less than $1.25/day), 70 percent of the global total. IFAD estimated that several hundred million more rural dwellers were just slightly less poor, living on less than $2 per day.[10] Table 2-1 underscores the deep poverty and low productivity that plague agriculture in low-income countries.[11]

Economic development involves people moving from subsistence farming and other low-productivity activities to higher-productivity activities in the manufacturing and services sectors.[12] But this structural transformation takes time, and the rural poor should not be left behind. Moreover, many developing countries have a comparative advantage in agriculture, and increased agricultural exports can help them address balance of payments problems, reduce debt burdens, and import the capital goods and technologies they need to move up the development ladder. Higher agricultural productivity, especially in Africa, is also a key to achieving food security for the global poor. Thus investments in rural areas and in raising smallholder productivity can make growth more pro-poor.[13]

Perhaps in part because of their low agricultural productivity, many

9. IFAD (2010); and Aksoy and Beghin (2005, p. 18).

10. IFAD (2010, annex 1).

11. The new IFAD (2016) report on rural development came out just as this volume was going to press. Unfortunately, the data on rural poverty are less detailed in the new report. The new report shows further progress in reducing rural poverty; however, since the regional aggregates are different, it is not possible to directly compare the new and old numbers.

12. IFAD (2016, Overview and synthesis).

13. IFAD (2016); and Timmer (2014).

Table 2-1   Key Agriculture and Poverty Indicators
for Select Country Groups, 2011

Indicator	Country groups		
Panel A	Low income	Lower middle	Upper middle
Rural population % of total population (n=138)	72	62	40
Agriculture value added per worker constant 2005 $ (n=108)	316	1,168	2,234
Agriculture, value added % of GDP (n=114)	34	18	9
Cereal yield (kg/ha) 2009–11 average (n=128)	1,587	3,080	4,664
Employment in agriculture % of total employment in 2005 (n=69)	76	50	37
Poverty headcount ratio at rural poverty line % of rural population (n=37)	50	26	34
Poverty headcount ratio at urban poverty line % of urban population (n=38)	26	14	17

Panel B	East Asia	South Asia	Sub-Saharan Africa	Other developing countries
Total population (millions)	1,349	1,616	777	1,497
Poverty headcount ratio at $2/day % of total population	36	71	76	30
Poverty headcount ratio at $1.25/day % of total population	16	39	53	11
Rural population (millions)	763	1,112	497	590
Rural poverty headcount ratio at $2/day % of rural population	35	80	87	39
Rural poverty headcount ratio at $1.25/day % of rural population	15	45	62	16

Sources: Panel A: World Bank's World Development Indicators; Panel B: 2011 Rural Poverty Report, United Nations International Fund for Agricultural Development.

Notes: Panel A: Figures represent population-weighted means; data for 2011, unless otherwise noted; number of countries in parentheses; Panel B: Data for 2008, or closest available year for 113 developing countries.

poor countries have yet to develop competitive manufacturing sectors, and they are relatively dependent on agricultural exports.[14] For low- and lower-middle-income countries, the share of agricultural products in total exports is two to three times that for upper-middle-income countries. Among the lowest-income countries, and excluding textile and apparel exports from Bangladesh and Cambodia, the average share of agriculture in total exports is nearly a third. Yet many developing country agricultural exports are at a disadvantage because of high-income country policies that limit market access and suppress global commodity prices, including for products such as sugar, cotton, and peanuts (chapter 3). Many other low-income country exports are tropical products (such as cocoa, coffee, and tea) that face relatively low tariffs when minimally processed. But industrialized countries often put higher tariffs on more processed products, which makes it hard for developing country exporters to add value and create jobs in downstream activities. For example, cocoa beans and cocoa paste face no duties in the U.S. market, but chocolate is subject to tariff-rate quotas that tightly restrict imports based on its sugar and dairy content.

Overall, the World Bank's *World Development Report 2008* found that growth in the agriculture sector in developing countries is at least twice as powerful in reducing poverty as growth in other sectors.[15] Thus, while the long-term goal of development is to move people out of agriculture, investments to improve smallholder productivity and to connect rural areas to urban markets can help ensure that the poorest people in the poorest countries are not left behind during the process.[16]

GLOBAL FOOD PRICES AND THE POOR

The relationship among prices, agricultural development, and food security is not simple.[17] In the early 2000s, prices hit a low point, and antipoverty campaigners targeted high-income country support for agriculture

14. Gelb and Diofasi (2015).
15. World Bank (2007, p. 30).
16. Timmer (2014).
17. Aksoy and Hoekman (2010); and Elliott (2006, chap. 4).

as a barrier to raising incomes for poor farmers. After the price spikes in the late 2000s, global concerns shifted to the problems that high prices created for the food security of the poor. But what was particularly harmful for the poor was the magnitude and speed of the price increases (figure 2-1). During the 2007–08 price spikes, wheat and maize prices roughly doubled in the span of two years, while rice prices tripled in just a few months.[18]

What matters for the poor over the longer term is whether and how the economy adjusts to food price changes. Most often, however, analysis of the impact of food prices on poverty focuses on the short run and uses a net benefit ratio approach pioneered by Angus Deaton.[19] This approach is based on the intuition that higher food prices tend to benefit poor households that are net food sellers and harm those that are net buyers of food. Thus, in the short run, the net impact of price fluctuations depends on the distribution of each type of household within and across developing countries.

With around half of the economically active population linked to agriculture in low- and middle-income countries in 2010 (just under 60 percent in sub-Saharan Africa), one might think that the net effect of higher food prices in these countries in the short run would be roughly zero.[20] But most studies find that many smallholder households are net buyers of food and that, overall, there are more net buyers than net sellers of food in most developing countries.[21] Thus, studies using the Deaton approach to simulate the effects of the 2007–08 price spikes concluded that there would be an increase in poverty of 100 million people or more.[22]

Even in the short run, some very poor countries could see net benefits from higher food prices. In Cambodia, for example, rice provides 65 percent of calories, on average, but most rural households own some land and Cambodia is a net rice exporter. Overall, Maltosoglou and others find that the average Cambodian household would gain from a 10 percent price increase, though urban households are a bit worse off, as are the relatively

18. Headey (2011, p. 1).
19. Deaton (1989).
20. FAO (2012a, p. 114, table A1).
21. Aksoy and Hoekman (2010).
22. Ivanic and Martin (2008); and de Hoyos and Medvedev (2009).

few rural households with no land. Ivanic and Martin also find net short-term benefits from higher prices for Cambodia, as well as for China, Vietnam, and Albania.[23]

In the medium to longer term, many more countries could benefit as higher prices encourage increased investment in the agriculture sector, which will increase producer incomes and create opportunities for some net buyers to become net sellers. Increased agricultural investments will also create demand for inputs and other complementary goods, which will increase demand for rural labor and contribute to rising wages. Aksoy and Isik-Dikmelik examine household surveys from nine low-income countries and find that about half of net buyers are marginal buyers. Moreover, households that are net buyers tend to be better off economically than net sellers. They conclude that,

> On average, only 8 percent of all households in the sample countries have income and food-buying characteristics that make them seriously vulnerable to food price increases.[24]

Ivanic and Martin use household surveys from a larger sample of 31 developing countries and link household models and economy-wide (general equilibrium) models to explore the long- and short-run effects of food price changes on poverty. Their simulations suggest that a 50 percent food price increase could reduce poverty among farmer-headed households by as much as 10 percent in the medium to long run, and among all rural households by around 7 percent. They find that, even with a doubling of food prices, poverty falls in the long run for all but urban households. There are differences at the individual country level, however. A 50 percent increase in food prices would decrease extreme poverty ($1.25 per day or less) in 15 of the 31 countries in the medium run and increase it by 0.5 percent or less in 8 countries. Poverty would increase by more than 1 percent in only 6 countries. In the long run, poverty would decline in 22 of 31 countries, but Indonesia, Nigeria, and Timor-Leste would see increases of 3 percent to 5 percent.[25]

---

23. Maltosglou and others (2010); and Ivanic and Martin (2014).

24. Aksoy and Isik-Dikmelik (2010, p. 115).

25. Ivanic and Martin (2014), where poverty reduction data come from tables 4, 5, and 6.

In an in-depth study of Uganda, using partial and general equilibrium methods, Campenhout, Pauw, and Minot also find that welfare increases and poverty declines for rural households in the long run.[26] Jacoby develops a simple theoretical model that allows for economy-wide adjustments to food price increases. Using data for India, Jacoby finds that, overall, rural wages rise by more than enough to compensate for consumption losses due to higher prices.[27] In the Indian context, in addition to higher demand for agricultural labor leading to higher wages, the competition for labor leads India's large service sector to also raise wages. Headey suggests that applying the Jacoby model to other developing countries would show benefits for those countries that, like India, have large shares of employment in agriculture and services. He uses cross-country data to examine "poverty episodes" of one to five years, and concludes that "on the whole increases in the real price of food tend to be poverty reducing."[28] Overall, he estimates that far from increasing poverty by 100 million or more, higher food prices might have reduced it by roughly that amount, though he again cautions that the pattern does not hold for every country in the sample.

Finally, there are concerns about the impact of higher food prices on the balance of payments for food-importing countries. Ng and Aksoy do find that more low-income countries are net *food* importers than exporters. But they also find that relatively more low-income countries are net exporters of *agricultural* commodities overall (including cotton and other agricultural raw materials). The authors also find that net food imports as a share of total imports in low-income countries, other than oil exporters and countries in conflict, are only around 2 percent on average. They conclude that some low-income countries did become more vulnerable as food prices rose in the mid-2000s, but that "[the] results do not indicate a very serious situation. The deterioration is about half a percent of GDP, on average, and relatively few countries are really vulnerable."[29]

In sum, higher food prices can put significant strains on poor house-

26. Campenhout, Pauw, and Minot (2013).

27. Jacoby (2013).

28. Headey (2014, p. 20).

29. Ng and Aksoy (2010, pp. 144–47); quotation is from p. 158.

holds, especially when prices increases are large and rapid. But the poorest households in developing countries are typically in rural areas and depend on agriculture for at least a portion of their income. Over the medium to longer run, many more of these households can benefit—and the overall net benefits will be positive for many countries—if governments allow global price increases to pass through to the domestic economy.

THE NEED FOR POLICY REFORM IN RICH AND POOR COUNTRIES

In sum, agriculture is an important sector for the poorest countries, and for the poor residing in them. The challenge for developing country policymakers is to balance the short-run impact on poor consumers against the need for prices high enough to encourage investments in productivity-improving technologies and management practices. Ng and Aksoy find that the higher agricultural prices of recent years had the desired effect of raising production in middle-income countries but generated a smaller supply response in low-income countries.[30] In those cases, governments and donors need to do more to improve the investment climate, ensure that smallholders have the tools they need to improve productivity, and invest in infrastructure to better connect rural to urban markets.

In the not-so-distant past, many developing country governments tilted in the opposite direction and taxed agriculture in order to subsidize urban consumers and manufacturing activities. Bilateral and multilateral donors also sharply reduced aid for the agricultural sector and rural development in the 1980s and 1990s, because such aid was seen as ineffective. Those policies are changing, however. Anderson, Rausser, and Swinnen show that, on average, developing country policies shifted from highly negative in earlier decades to slightly positive support for the agricultural sector in more recent years. Donors and politicians alike have come to realize that investments in agriculture can contribute to "pro-poor" growth that causes the poverty rate to decline faster than it otherwise might.[31]

---

30. Ng and Aksoy (2010).

31. Anderson, Rausser, and Swinnen (2013, p. 51). For an extensive review, see the World Bank's 2008 *World Development Report* and the sources cited therein; see also Timmer (2005).

Despite increasing aid for agriculture in developing countries, most donor countries maintain traditional subsidies for their own farmers. Those subsidies distort decisions about which commodities to plant where, increase uncertainty about future prices and, at the margin, reduce incentives to invest in developing country agriculture. Biofuel policies have the opposite effect on prices, but they still distort decisions on where and in what commodities to invest. Thus, advanced country policies, including those of the United States, are often at cross purposes, and foreign assistance is less effective than it could be in helping poor countries use agriculture to reduce poverty and promote food security.

3

DOMESTIC AGRICULTURAL SUPPORT AT THE EXPENSE OF DEVELOPING COUNTRY FARMERS

AS THE NEW MILLENNIUM WAS arriving, subsidies and trade barriers in rich countries were helping to drive agricultural prices to historic lows. Oxfam launched its "Make Trade Fair" campaign to highlight the harm done to struggling farmers in developing countries as a result of industrialized countries transferring hundreds of billions of dollars to their relatively well-off farmers. The level of government support fell, mostly automatically, as prices rose in the late 2000s. But food prices began falling again in 2013, and the trade-distorting policies that remain in high-income countries, along with new policies in emerging powers, could once again become major distortions in global markets.

Slashing trade-distorting agricultural subsidies was a central goal when the World Trade Organization (WTO) launched the Doha Round of negotiations in 2001. Unfortunately, deep disagreements over agriculture and other issues repeatedly blocked progress, and the negotiations collapsed in 2008. WTO members did manage to agree on a few items to reduce agricultural distortions at ministerial meetings in recent years, notably including the elimination of export subsidies. But the 2015 WTO meeting in Nairobi also effectively ended the Doha Round without providing clear guidance for new ways forward on agriculture—or anything else.

Owing to subsidies and trade barriers in the United States and other countries, farmers in these countries continue to produce subsidized crops when market prices would have signaled that they should be reconsidering their planting decisions. This market distortion further suppresses global prices and pushes the full burden of adjustment onto producers in developing countries whose governments cannot afford subsidies or choose not to use them. Consequently, poor farmers in developing countries—most of whom have neither savings nor safety nets—risk falling further into poverty. The global market distortions associated with protectionist agricultural policies also discourage investments in developing country agriculture for the future.

The United States is by no means the worst offender when it comes to subsidizing its farmers, but in recent years it has missed crucial opportunities to lead reform efforts. As one of the largest producers and exporters of corn, wheat, oilseeds, and meat, U.S. policies have large effects on global markets. The most recent farm bill, passed by Congress in 2014, included some market-oriented changes but still provided billions of dollars in market-distorting subsidies. It also diverged from the framework for reform embodied in international trade rules. And during the WTO ministerial meeting in Nairobi, U.S. negotiators blocked new disciplines on export finance and food aid because of opposition from key domestic constituencies.

This chapter will review trends in support for agriculture across the industrialized countries and examine their effects on farmers in developing countries. The European Union, a major player in global agricultural markets, provides high levels of support to its farmers and EU barriers to imports are still quite high in many sectors. Nonetheless, EU policymakers have at least made a concerted effort to make agricultural support less trade-distorting than before. U.S. agricultural support policies, by contrast, are more complicated, and the fact that overall levels of support are lower today has little to do with changes in policy.

U.S. food aid programs, which grew out of past policies supporting American farmers, are an area where U.S. reform could have immediate and significant benefits for the most vulnerable of the global poor, and where U.S. policies are most clearly in conflict. The U.S. approach to food aid remains rooted in an era when the government propped up prices, in part, by buying and storing crops when surpluses emerged. Diverting some of these surpluses for food aid was a way to reduce the costs of those policies. Even though the government long ago scrapped most supply controls, Congress still requires that most U.S. food aid be purchased domestically and transported to its destination on U.S.-flagged ships. These requirements make food aid far costlier, and mean that the U.S. food aid budget does not stretch as far as it could and is less timely in emergencies. Providing in-kind food aid also undercuts the goals of the primary U.S. foreign assistance initiative for global food security, Feed the Future, which aims to build up the agriculture sector in developing countries so they can feed themselves.

Finally, while U.S. and other industrialized country policies still need reform, most developing countries have few international constraints on their actions in the agricultural sector. Some emerging markets, including China and India, are sharply increasing government support for agriculture and could become new sources of global market instability. American producers are increasingly concerned about the impact of this trend on U.S. exports, but other countries are unlikely to follow "do as I say, not as I do" advice from U.S. policymakers. The concluding section of this chapter looks at how the WTO could help to strengthen international disciplines on agricultural policies and prevent a new outbreak of costly "subsidy wars."

THE LANDSCAPE OF AGRICULTURAL SUPPORT
20 YEARS AFTER THE URUGUAY ROUND

Agricultural trade and other policies are an anomaly in high-income countries around the world. Tariffs on agriculture tend to be substantially higher than for other products, and the international trade rules permit the use of quantitative restrictions and subsidies that are barred for manufactured goods.[1] A World Bank database of overall assistance to agriculture in 82 countries over more than five decades shows that it has

---

1. Elliott (2015a).

declined in high-income countries since the mid-1980s. But, according to these estimates, support for agriculture in high-income countries started out well above protection for other goods and, even with the recent declines in support, the *relative* rate of assistance to agriculture was actually a bit higher in 2005–10 than it was in the late 1950s.[2] Meanwhile, agricultural support in some developing countries is rising in both relative and absolute terms. The most recent monitoring report from the Organization for Economic Cooperation and Development (OECD) finds that average support in the emerging economies "increased from very low or even negative levels to approach the average level of OECD countries."[3]

The decline in support to agricultural producers in high-income countries is not all due to changes in policy, however.[4] The increase in commodity prices that began in the early 2000s reduced the value of countercyclical support whether governments embraced reform or not. Some countries did adopt less trade-distorting policies that decouple payments from production and prices. The EU moved in this direction and, while the volume of support remains relatively high, the share that is trade-distorting is down sharply over the past decade. U.S. agricultural support levels are still lower than in Europe and most other OECD countries, and they are far lower than in the late 1990s. But the decline is mainly because most U.S. farm programs are countercyclical and subsidies fell automatically as prices rose. Across the OECD as a whole, levels of and trends in support to agriculture vary widely.[5]

In addition to the mixed reform record, it is important to note that even where reforms took place, such as in the EU, an array of border measures remain in place to restrict imports of agricultural products.[6] Most high-income countries waive these restrictions for the United Nations (UN)–designated least developed countries (LDCs) under duty-free, quota-free

2. Anderson, Rausser, and Swinnen (2013, figure 2).

3. OECD (2016, p. 44).

4. Ibid., p. 42.

5. For a detailed review of agricultural policies in the EU and other selected OECD countries, including the United States, see European Parliament (2012). Anderson, Rausser, and Swinnen (2013) explore the trends in agricultural support and the political economy of reform.

6. Bureau, Laborde, and Orden (2013).

trade preference programs like the EU's Everything But Arms initiative. Yet some of these programs exclude sensitive items, such as dairy and poultry products in Canada and rice and sugar in Japan. Only the United States has refused to implement duty-free, quota-free market access for all LDCs. Under the Africa Growth and Opportunity Act, the United States provides nearly complete duty-free market access for poorer countries in sub-Saharan Africa, but even that program excludes sugar, dairy, chocolate and other confectionary goods, peanuts, tobacco, and other sensitive agricultural products.[7]

Bilateral and regional trade agreements, such as the recently concluded Trans-Pacific Partnership (TPP), also often leave barriers to imports of the most sensitive agricultural products in place. Neither the United States nor the EU has thus far been willing to constrain its domestic subsidy policies in regional or bilateral agreements.[8] Moreover, in the TPP negotiations, the larger, richer countries were able to negotiate better market access arrangements for their agricultural products than Vietnam, the poorest of the parties to the deal by far.[9] Thus, while regional arrangements are reducing barriers to agricultural trade, they are not a substitute for nondiscriminatory, multilateral negotiations.

Subsidies and Overall Support
The OECD has been collecting and publishing detailed estimates of the size and composition of support to agricultural producers since the mid-1980s. Figure 3-1 shows the OECD estimates of producer support as a percent of gross farm receipts (including the value of the support) for high-income OECD members from 1986 to 2014. The average annual value of that support in 2012–14 was $250 billion, a bit below the peak of $279 billion in 2004. As a share of gross farm receipts, however, producer support declined to 17 percent, less than half of peak levels in the mid-1980s.

Within the overall OECD average, there are wide differences in levels of producer support and countries tend to cluster broadly into two groups. At the top of figure 3-1 are uncompetitive, food-importing countries from

7. CGD Working Group on Global Trade Preference Reform (2010); and Elliott (2014).
8. See Hendrix and Kotschwar (2016) for analysis of the TPP agreement on agriculture.
9. Elliott (2016).

Figure 3-1   Estimated Government Support to Producers, 1986–2014

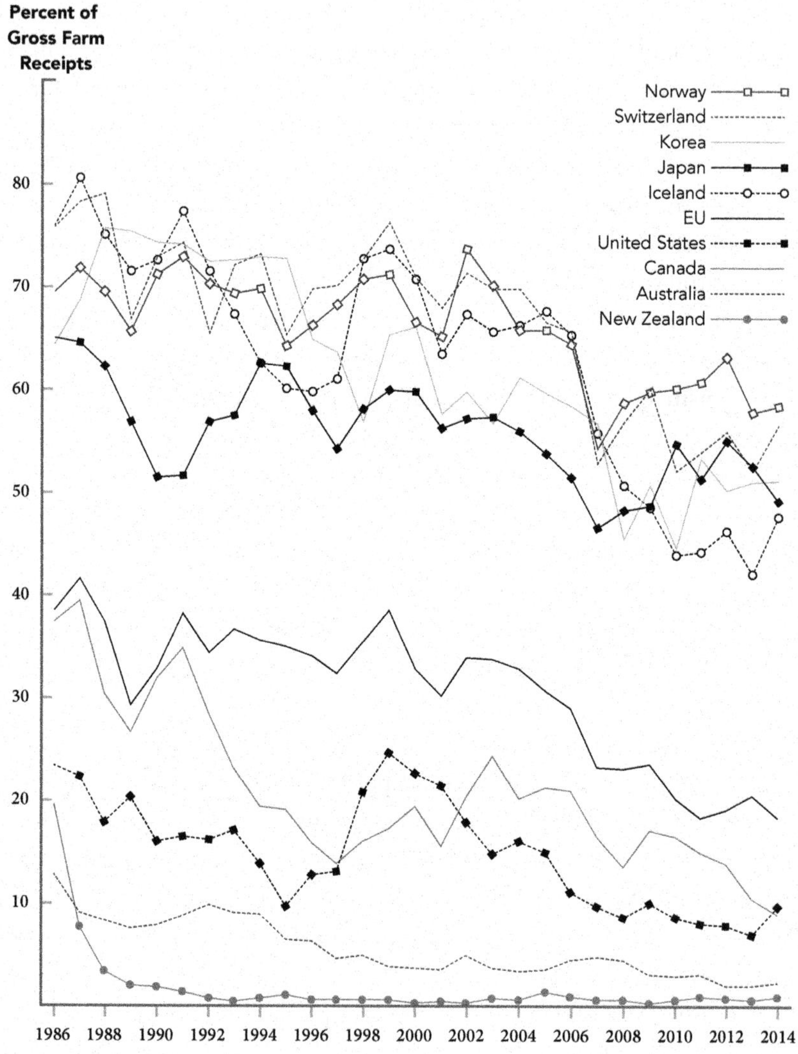

**Percent of
Gross Farm
Receipts**

Source: Organization for Economic Cooperation and Development (OECD), Producer and Consumer Support database (accessed May 2016).

northern Europe and northeastern Asia that heavily protect farmers at levels well above the OECD average. At the very bottom are Australia and New Zealand, highly competitive exporters of a range of agricultural commodities that adopted reforms and mostly eliminated producer support long ago. The EU, Canada, and the United States are in between, though the EU level of support remains almost twice as high as that for the United States.

Members of the General Agreement on Tariffs and Trade (GATT; the WTO's predecessor) signed the Uruguay Round agreement, including the Agreement on Agriculture (URAA), in 1994. The URAA identified three types of agricultural support that should be reduced: domestic support, tariffs and other trade barriers, and export subsidies. The agreement further divided domestic support into three boxes: amber for the most trade-distorting forms (those linked to current prices and production); blue for subsidies that are linked to current prices but have production-limiting features; and green for minimally distorting forms of support, which were not subject to ceilings or reduction requirements.[10] The initial aim of the Doha Round was to build on this framework and further reduce the ceilings for trade-distorting support and trade barriers.

Under the URAA, WTO members are supposed to report on policies in all of the support categories, but there are often long lags and reporting inconsistencies.[11] The OECD definition of what constitutes the most trade-distorting forms of support, as well as its measurement methods, do not match up exactly with those of the WTO. The OECD measures are consistently calculated and available for a longer period than the WTO notifications, and are more up to date.[12] They therefore give a better sense of the trends in support to the agriculture sector, and some indication of the commitment to reform across countries. The OECD estimates also are more closely linked to current market conditions. In particular, for political and negotiating reasons, the WTO measures support for com-

10. See Elliott (2006, pp. 17–18), for a brief summary of the agreement, and see the WTO website on "The Uruguay Round reform programme for trade in agriculture" for more detailed information: www.wto.org/english/tratop_e/agric_e/ag_intro00_contents_e.htm.

11. Many countries—and not just poorer ones—do not fulfill these obligations on a timely basis. Moreover, the vagueness of the rules in many cases makes the economic impact of the data in the notifications difficult to interpret. For analysis of key countries' compliance with WTO commitments, including questionable measures that are not reported to the WTO, see Orden, Blandford, and Josling (2011).

12. The OECD (2016, p. 47) defines the most distorting supports as market price support (typically enforced through trade barriers), payments linked to commodity output, and unconstrained payments for variable input use, such as energy subsidies.

modity prices using historical reference prices from the late 1980s. The OECD measure of price support uses current market prices and therefore is better for getting a sense of the actual economic impact of these policies.

Using the OECD numbers, figure 3-2 provides some indication of how much of the decline in producer support has been associated with policy reforms, though price changes also affect the value of output-based support. Korea and Japan most clearly demonstrate the limits of the URAA. They are among those providing the largest amounts of support overall and they still provide most of it in highly trade-distorting forms. When the URAA went into effect, Iceland reformed support for sheep meat by replacing output-based payments with payments based on historical numbers of animals, making this type of support somewhat less trade-distorting. Yet as figures 3-1 and 3-2 show, Iceland is still among the countries providing the most support. Canada removed market price support for grains in the mid-1990s, but it maintains tight supply management policies for dairy, poultry, and eggs. Subsequent fluctuations in Canadian support are mainly due to fluctuations in the prices of those products, especially dairy. Norway and Switzerland still provide some of the highest levels of support overall, but they have steadily moved toward less-distorting forms of support. Still, government support accounts for more than half of gross farm gate receipts (figure 3-1) and much of it is still in trade-distorting forms, including high trade barriers.

The most striking shift in figure 3-2 is the fall in EU trade-distorting support from more than 90 percent of the total in the 1980s to around a quarter by 2014. The EU, confronted with budget pressures and an expanding membership, reformed the Common Agricultural Policy (CAP) to make it less costly and less trade-distorting (see box 3-1). Nevertheless, the EU still provides around €80 billion annually in producer support. That amount is surely large enough to affect production decisions by "easing credit constraints, and lowering risk aversion" for farmers.[13] EU trade barriers are also still relatively high, and many exporters, notably in the United States, view European product standards as being set higher than necessary to ensure food safety.

The share of U.S. support that is most distorting generally has been

---

13. Orden (2013, p. 9); see also Bureau, Laborde, and Orden (2013, pp. 62–66).

Figure 3-2   The Most Trade-Distorting Forms of
Agricultural Producer Support, 1986–2014

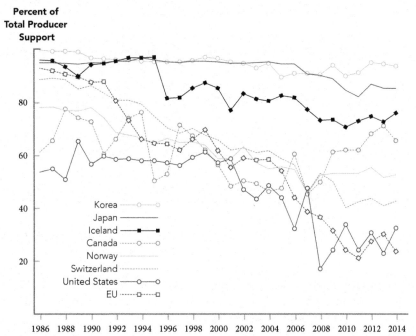

**Percent of
Total Producer
Support**

80

60

40

20

Korea
Japan
Iceland
Canada
Norway
Switzerland
United States
EU

1986   1988   1990   1992   1994   1996   1998   2000   2002   2004   2006   2008   2010   2012   2014

Source: OECD, Producer and Consumer Support database (accessed May 2016).

Note: Output-based support and payments based on unconstrained variable input use.

lower than that in other OECD countries, but, after making some reforms
to farm policies in the 1980s and 1990s, the decline in the share of trade-
distorting support in the 2000s was mostly attributable to rising agricultural prices. (The 2007–08 volatility is due mainly to fluctuating dairy
prices and policies.) After an attempt at more fundamental reform in the
mid-1990s, U.S. policy has been mixed at best, as discussed in the following section.

One noteworthy change in the composition of support is that, as out-
put-linked subsidies came down, input subsidies became relatively more
important in some countries. Agricultural production in rich countries is
highly mechanized, uses lots of fertilizer and other inputs, and is highly
energy-intensive. It is particularly perverse, then, that some countries, including the United States and the members of the EU, subsidize energy

Box 3-1   European Union CAP Reform

THE EU'S COMMON AGRICULTURAL POLICY (CAP) originally relied on trade barriers and supply management to support market prices. But the high level of intervention prices led to growing surpluses that had to be stored or disposed of on global markets with the help of export subsidies. By the mid-1980s, the costs of the CAP had led to budget pressures and trade tensions that could no longer be ignored. Pressures for reform continued into the early 1990s because of the need to open up space for EU negotiators to make concessions in the Uruguay Round of trade negotiations, and then into the 2000s because of the need to integrate new members from Eastern Europe without breaking the budget.[a]

CAP reforms to date follow a relatively consistent pattern of lower intervention prices combined with payments to farmers that are increasingly decoupled from current production.[b] As shown in the figure opposite, initial reforms involved modest reductions in market price support and increased payments based on historical acres or numbers of animals, making them partially decoupled from current production. Then, in 2004, overall support levels began dropping sharply as market prices rose, intervention prices were cut, and the partially decoupled payments were replaced with a "single farm payment" for income support that is independent of current production and prices. The EU reports those payments to the WTO in the green box.

In June 2013, representatives of member states and the European Parliament agreed to a CAP reform that makes 30 percent of the single farm payments (now the basic payment scheme) conditional on environmental performance and eliminates production (but not import) quotas for sugar (2017) and milk (2015). Farm groups and their political allies, however, are not giving up the fight for some traditional forms of support. The latest CAP revision, which was delayed by budget fights, grants some flexibility to member states that want to use a portion of CAP funds to continue providing some coupled support for particular commodities. Further provisions are aimed at making payments more equitable both across and within member states.[c]

While farmers do not have to produce anything to receive what is now called basic payment, most still do. CAP programs clearly are less distorting

Composition of EU Support to Producers, 1986–2014

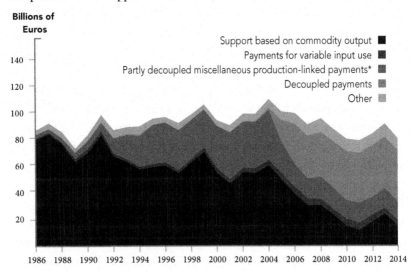

Source: OECD Producer and Consumer Support database (accessed October 2015).

*Payments based on current area, animal numbers, receipts or income, production required.

today, but they are still worth nearly €80 billion and account for 20 percent of gross farm receipts in recent years. Even if the links between programs and production continue to weaken, support of that magnitude reduces risk and eases credit constraints for farmers. Paradoxically, the level of support in the EU is also likely larger than what it would be had there been no reform, since rising prices would have reduced the amount of market price support and export subsidies needed to maintain internal prices. But the level of *distorting* support would also be higher than what it is today, unless authorities had been willing to simply cut farmers off.

a. Anderson, Rausser, and Swinnen (2013, pp. 21–22, 28).
b. Elliott (2006, pp. 38–40); OECD (2012, chap. 7).
c. See European Commission (2013).

use in agriculture. In the United States, tax rebates for on-farm fuel use reportedly amounted to $2.5 billion in 2014, but that figure has not been updated in years and the notes accompanying the U.S. OECD estimates concede that the data are problematic.[14] In the EU, fuel tax rebates averaging more than $3 billion annually were the second-largest category of direct payments after decoupled income support, ahead of environmental payments.[15]

In sum, while producer support is generally declining across the more advanced members of the OECD, the degree to which those declines are due to policy reform rather than higher prices varies widely.[16] Moreover, even where there has been significant subsidy reform, as in the EU, trade barriers remain high for many agricultural and food products that developing countries might otherwise export.

Trade Barriers and Commodity-Specific Support

Almost everywhere, average tariffs are higher for agricultural than for industrial products and agricultural products are more likely to be subject to abnormally high tariff peaks.[17] Many countries also still use tariff-rate quotas to protect sensitive farm products, though the WTO prohibits quantitative restrictions for industrial products.[18] Even now, with higher prices and whatever reforms have taken place, agricultural trade barriers remain mostly unchanged from where the Uruguay Round left them, at least in the high-income countries.

All too often, the most highly protected commodities in high-income countries are products in which lower-income countries otherwise would have a comparative advantage. The most highly supported product across the OECD on average is rice, but this support is concentrated in Japan and Korea, where the barriers are exceptionally high. High levels of support for sugar occur mainly in Japan, Europe, and the United States. Poor

---

14. See page 6 of the OECD report at www.oecd.org/tad/agricultural-policies/USA_cookbook.pdf (accessed November 3, 2015).

15. European Parliament (2012, p. 93).

16. Anderson, Raausser, and Swinnen (2013, p. 30).

17. Elliott (2015) provides a brief summary of the international trade rules for agriculture.

18. Tariff-rate quotas allow a designated amount of imports to enter at a low tariff rate, with imports above that level subject to much higher, often prohibitive, tariffs.

countries would particularly benefit from trade liberalization for these commodities. In the more protectionist countries at the top of figures 3-1 and 3-2, uncompetitive farmers tend to receive support for whatever they produce. Thus, Japan, Norway, and Switzerland all have average tariffs on nonagricultural products of 2 percent to 3 percent, but averages of 19 percent, 51 percent, and 36 percent, respectively, on agricultural goods. Moreover, even higher tariff peaks are hidden in those averages.[19]

Turning to commodity-specific support in the two largest markets, table 3-1 shows the value of commodity-specific support, including the effect of trade barriers, as a share of gross farm receipts in the United States and the EU. In the United States, the average tariff is twice as high for agriculture as for other products, while in Europe it is three times as high. In both these markets, only agricultural products have tariffs that reach 100 percent and above.[20] The United States provides the most support to certain "white products": sugar, cotton, dairy, and in some years rice. The EU used to provide even higher levels of support for sugar, but it reduced them, in part in response to a challenge under international trade rules.[21] While subsidized EU sugar exports dropped as a result, and LDCs and certain other developing countries have preferential access to the EU market, tariff-rate quotas remain in place to manage imports from others. These days, the EU's highest levels of support and import protection are for meat, especially beef. In addition to meat and sugar, the EU restricts imports of a wide range of products, including fruits and vegetables. Besides sugar and dairy, the United States also has highly restrictive tariff-rate quotas and tariff peaks on imports of peanuts and tobacco.

Experience with domestic reforms in some of these sectors suggests that these barriers will not come down unless WTO members can reach agreement to do so as part of a global bargain. When the EU and the United States decided (for different reasons) to reform their price support

19. WTO/ITC/UNCTAD (2014).

20. In this discussion, average tariffs include estimates of the ad valorem equivalent of other border measures, including tariff-rate quotas, specific duties (a set value per unit of imports), and compound tariffs (combining ad valorem tariffs and specific duties). See Elliott (2006, chap. 2) for an in-depth discussion of the range of measures that countries use to support and protect agriculture.

21. Agrosynergie (2011, pp. 3–4).

Table 3-1   Commodity-Specific Transfers from
Government to Producers, Average 2012–14

Commodity	Percent of gross farm receipts	
	United States	European Union
Rice	2	0
Sugar	17	11
Cotton	10	N/A
Poultry	0	15
Beef and veal	0	32
Sheep meat	9	10
Pork	0	1
Milk	11	2
Maize	4	0
Wheat	7	2
Soybeans	3	0
Other grains	6	0
Average	6	7

Source: OECD Producer and Consumer Support database (accessed October 2015).

Note: Other grains include barley, oats, and sorghum.

programs for sugar (EU) and for tobacco and peanuts (U.S.), domestic supply controls were lifted but restrictions on imports were not.

Emerging Market Farm Policies

The large emerging powers are a growing force in global markets, yet the WTO places few disciplines on their agricultural policies. It is no longer possible to ignore what is happening with producer support in these countries. The OECD provides estimates for newer OECD members and for some important emerging markets that are not yet members, including China but not (yet) India. With relatively few constraints under the Uruguay Round agreement, some developing countries have ramped up that support in ways that introduce significant new distortions in global markets. Because of its sheer size and growth, China alone now accounts for almost half of total support to agriculture across the 50 countries that the OECD is monitoring, up from less than 5 percent in the mid-1990s.[22]

Until the 1990s, developing countries generally taxed the agriculture sector, either directly through export taxes on cash crops or indirectly by favoring the industrial sector and urban consumers. The so-called real rate of assistance moved from strongly negative in the 1960s across all regions of the developing world to roughly neutral in Latin America and sub-Saharan Africa and mildly positive in Asia by the early 2000s.[23] Available calculations from the OECD show producer support in some large emerging markets that is close to or even above the average level for the advanced OECD members (figure 3-3). India, to date, has not cooperated with the OECD to produce similar calculations, but the figure shows a rough estimate based on the most recent available WTO notifications.

Overall, producer support as a share of gross farm receipts tends to fluctuate significantly in many of these economies and it is difficult to detect clear trends.[24] On the good-news side of the ledger, Brazil, Chile, and South Africa are competitive agricultural exporters where support generally has been declining; since 2010, support amounted to 5 percent or less of farm receipts in those countries. Turkey and Russia have been fluctuating around the OECD average. Mexico's support to producers fell sharply in the first half of the 2000s and then leveled off below 15 percent for the past decade.

The worrisome trend, given its size, is the sharply increasing level of support in China, which surpassed OECD levels in recent years. Though these levels dropped sharply, and market price support turned negative during the price spikes in 2008, the OECD estimates show that China's producer support increased from an average of 380 billion yuan in 2005–07 to 1,800 billion yuan ($290 billion) in 2014. Market price support, one of the more trade-distorting categories, accounted for just under half of total producer support in the earlier period and rose to 80 percent in 2014 ($240 billion). China's most recent WTO notification is for 2010 and shows negligible levels of market price support, at least in part because of

22. Anderson, Rausser, and Swinnen (2013); and OECD (2016, p. 40).

23. Anderson, Rausser, and Swinnen (2013, pp. 52–53).

24. Indonesia and Ukraine also provide data to the OECD, but they are excluded from the discussion because the data are even more volatile.

Figure 3-3   Estimates of Government Support to Producers in Major
Emerging Market Economies, 2000 to Most Recent Available

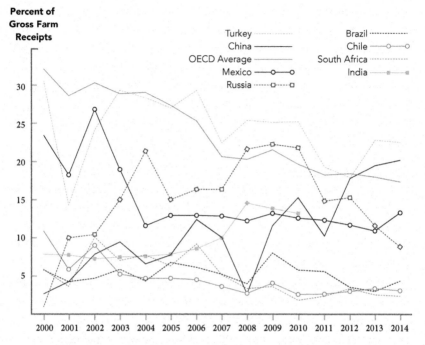

Notes: Data for India are estimated from India's most recent WTO notifications on domestic
support and FAO Stat data on production; available up to 2010. Source for other countries
is the OECD Producer and Consumer Support database; available up to 2014 (accessed May
2016).

peculiarities in the WTO rules about how to calculate support.[25] Using
the OECD numbers for total producer support, the figure in 2014 was
almost 3 percent of China's gross domestic product that year. In September
2016, the Obama administration requested formal consultations with
China at the WTO over its agricultural subsidies. This could be important
litigation to clarify how the URAA rules apply to developing countries.

Unfortunately, there are no OECD producer support estimates for
India, and its last WTO notification was in 2014 for the 2004–05 to
2010–11 marketing years. India, which reports in U.S. dollars rather than

25. Glauber (2016a) discusses how the WTO calculates market price support and why it
does not necessarily reflect current market conditions.

the local currency, provided almost $25 billion in green box subsidies, roughly four times higher than it reported for 2004–05. The report lists $5.6 billion for research, $3.3 billion for concessional loans and debt relief, and nearly $14 billion for public stockholding. India also reported providing $29 billion in input subsidies and a bit over $2 billion in market price support for rice, all up sharply from earlier years. DTB Associates LLP (2013) calculates a much higher figure for Indian market price support, and the peculiarities in WTO rules for this calculation make it difficult to know the true economic value of this support.[26] What we do know is that India's own reported spending on agriculture, like China's, increased sharply in recent years and totaled roughly 3 percent of its GDP in recent years.

THE MIXED REFORM RECORD OF U.S. AGRICULTURAL POLICY

In contrast to the relatively straightforward story in Europe of moving from highly distorting market interventions to mostly decoupled income support (box 3-1), the evolution of American farm policy is more complicated. Congress moved in a direction similar to that of the EU in the mid-1990s, consistent with the Uruguay Round agreement and at a time of high commodity prices. It quickly reversed course when prices fell, however (figure 3-4). The most recent farm legislation, passed in 2014, included measures that move some U.S. programs in a more market-oriented direction, or at least made them somewhat less trade-distorting. But it did not take long for complaints to arise that the 2014 bill did not do enough to protect farmers from price declines, and the partial reforms in it could well be reversed, just as the 1990s effort was. Even with those market-oriented reforms, the overall direction of recent U.S. farm bills has been away from the framework contained in the Uruguay Round agreement—a fact that poses challenges for U.S. leadership at the WTO.

---

26. Elliott (2015a).

Figure 3-4   Composition of U.S. Government Support to Producers, 1986–2014

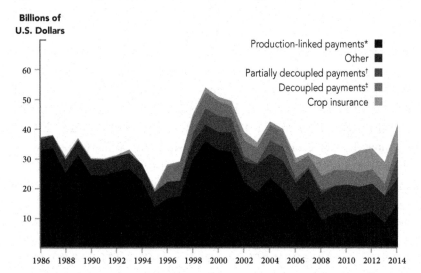

Source: OECD Producer and Consumer Support database (accessed October 2015).

*These include support based on commodity outputs; payments based on variable input use; and other production-linked payments which are based on current area, animal numbers, receipts or income, production required.

†Payments based on noncurrent animal numbers, receipts or income, production not required, less decoupled payments, tobacco and peanut buyouts.

‡These include direct payments (which are allotted to farmers that grow an eligible crop regardless of the price) and production flexibility contract (PFC) payments.

A Brief History of U.S. Farm Policy[27]

Government support to help American farmers by propping up prices began during the Great Depression, and the policies were highly interventionist. Congressional legislation set minimum prices for commodities and maintained them through import restrictions, as well as land idling schemes and government stockholding mechanisms to control domestic supplies. Congress began adjusting U.S. farm policies in the 1960s to con-

27. Orden, Paarlberg, and Roe (1999) analyze the economics and politics of U.S. farm policy from the 1930s to the late 1990s in great detail. Glauber and Effland (2016) succinctly summarize the full history, from the founding of the republic to the most recent farm bill; see also Elliott (2006, chap. 3) and Barnett, Coble, and Mercier (2016, pp. 42–44) for brief summaries.

trol budgetary expenditures and to improve export competitiveness for certain crops. Congress adopted further reforms in the 1980s that continued the move away from supply controls to support prices, and toward price-linked subsidies that supported revenues while allowing farmers to export at world prices. Note, however, that these market-oriented reforms did not apply to globally uncompetitive crops, such as sugar, dairy, tobacco, and peanuts, all of which are still protected behind high trade barriers.[28]

Figure 3-4 illustrates the shifts in the level and type of support to U.S. farmers from the mid-1980s when the OECD began compiling these data. The sharp dip in 1995 is the result of both high prices, which reduced the need for countercyclical subsidies, and a farm bill that continued the movement toward more market-oriented policies. The 1996 legislation kept the marketing loan program, which provides payments based on crop output when prices fall below a statutory floor price. Congress eliminated supply controls as a means of propping up prices for most products, as well as payments based on the difference between market prices and target prices for eligible commodities.[29] Instead, Congress provided decoupled direct payments that were based on the number of acres planted with eligible crops in the past and with no requirement for current production of those crops. Congress designed these payments to provide income support to farmers with minimal impacts on production decisions. The 1996 farm bill also continued premium subsidies to encourage farmers to buy crop insurance with the aim of reducing pressure on Congress to provide ad hoc emergency assistance in response to natural or other disasters.

As Orden, Paarlberg, and Roe describe, congressional enthusiasm for agricultural reform was never as great as the 1996 legislation suggested, and it did not take long to dissipate.[30] The surge in support in the late 1990s (figure 3-4) was due partly to the program's continuation of floor

---

28. Later reforms did remove domestic production quotas for tobacco and peanuts in exchange for other types of payments: see Orden (2005). The dairy program has also moved away from domestic supply controls, but continues to be complex and highly interventionist.

29. These countercyclical payments were paid on only 85 percent of base-year acreage and fixed yields, which made them partially decoupled from current production.

30. Orden, Paarlberg, and Roe (1999).

prices, which kicked in when prices fell, and partly to new interventions. When a combination of sharply falling prices and natural disasters hit in the late 1990s, Congress responded, as it had in the past, with emergency relief for farmers. Then, with prices still low, it formally reversed course in the 2002 farm bill and restored partially decoupled payments based on the difference between current market prices and legislatively set target prices. These new countercyclical payments were somewhat less distorting than the version eliminated in 1996 because, in addition to being based on historical acres, they did not require current production of covered crops. There was a surplus at the time of the 2002 farm bill, which made it easier for Congress to add the new countercyclical payments on top of the completely decoupled direct payments created by the 1996 bill.

The 2008 farm bill continued these programs with minor tweaks, while continuing to increase subsidies for crop insurance premiums. Rising commodity prices in this period meant that price-linked subsidies fell sharply while the role of crop insurance (barely visible in figure 3-4 prior to this) grew equally sharply. Higher prices leading to larger loss claims explains part of the increase. However, the insurance purchase subsidy to farmers also increased markedly over the years, rising to an average of $6.3 billion per year in 2008–14. Net insurance payments varied between $6.4 billion and $13.3 billion in 2011–13, well above the average of $2.5 billion over the previous three years.[31]

The 2014 Farm Bill

The 2014 farm bill was influenced by two key factors: real prices that were still higher than they had been since the 1970s (see figure 2-1) and pressure to cut the budget. As discussion of a new farm bill began, Congress was in the midst of a fierce political fight over cutting the deficit that included a near default on U.S. public debt in 2011 and a two-week government shutdown in 2013. The pressure to find savings in all parts of the budget, including the farm bill, was intense. With commodity prices and farm incomes at relatively high levels, the $5 billion in decoupled direct payments that farmers were receiving every year, regardless of market conditions, became politically untenable. Moreover, since the Doha Round of trade

---

31. Zulauf and Orden (2015, p. 2; and 2016, p. 256).

negotiations had collapsed in 2008, the constraints on policy from that source were weak at best.

Congress ultimately claimed $50 billion in savings in the farm bill, primarily by eliminating the decoupled direct payments, but those savings did not go back to taxpayers. Rather, Congress shifted 70 percent of the savings to new commodity programs while adding $6 billion in additional subsidies for new insurance programs over ten years.[32] From an international perspective, the new programs were only partially decoupled and thus relatively more trade-distorting than the direct payments they replaced. This result is unlikely to lead to a WTO challenge of U.S. policies in the short run, but it will constrain what the United States can offer in future negotiations.[33]

At the end of the day, the 2014 farm bill took a step in the direction of greater market orientation but was not a sharp departure from previous policy.[34] It preserved the marketing loan program to keep a floor under eligible commodity prices and bolstered crop insurance. It also, just barely, delivered on a promise to "end payments to millionaires." Operations with an adjusted gross income (including nonfarm income) of $900,000 or more are not eligible for payments, though operators may find ways around the cap.[35]

The major new commodity program is the Agriculture Risk Coverage (ARC) program, which compensates for revenue shortfalls arising from falls in either yield or price. It uses a moving average of recent national market prices and county-specific crop yields to calculate the benchmark revenue against which shortfalls are measured. This feature makes the program more market-oriented than programs with statutorily fixed reference prices because the benchmark will move with the market, albeit

32. The Congressional Budget Office (CBO) scoring for the farm bill as it emerged from the House-Senate conference is available on the CBO website at www.cbo.gov/sites/default/files/cbofiles/attachments/hr2642LucasLtr.pdf (accessed October 30, 2015).

33. Cotton is a potential exception to this assertion, as discussed below.

34. A more detailed description and analysis of the new farm bill is in Zulauf and Orden (2016) and in various briefs from the University of Illinois' Farmdoc Daily website, http://farmdocdaily.illinois.edu/. Summary and analysis of the legislation is also available from the U.S. Department of Agriculture (USDA) Economic Research Service at http://www.ers.usda.gov/agricultural-act-of-2014-highlights-and-implications.aspx (accessed July 13, 2016).

35. Congressional Research Service (2014, pp. 55–56).

more gradually. Under pressure from commodity groups, however, Congress also set a floor below which the average price in the benchmark calculation cannot fall.[36]

These changes were not enough for some, however, and even though the 2014 farm bill eliminated the partially decoupled countercyclical payments, it brought back a very similar program under a different name. Southern producers of rice and peanuts had been relatively more dependent on the countercyclical and direct payments, and they wanted more protection against sustained low prices than what ARC would provide. Direct payments per acre for peanuts and rice under previous farm bills were far higher than for other crops and producers of these crops also received countercyclical payments in more years than other crops.[37] Congress responded by giving farmers the option to choose either ARC or a new Price Loss Coverage (PLC) program. As with the earlier countercyclical payments, PLC provides payments when market prices fall below legislatively set target levels, which Congress also raised from their previous levels.

Both the PLC and ARC programs are partially decoupled because they are paid on 85 percent of acres planted with eligible program commodities in a historical base period. For the PLC program, the crop yields used for the payment calculation are also based on an historic average. But the farm bill allowed farmers to reallocate base acres across commodities and to update yields to a more recent period, so anticipation of future updating opportunities could affect planting decisions. The addition of fixed reference price floors in the ARC also undermined the move toward increased market orientation in that program.

The legislation also required farmers to choose between the ARC and PLC programs, and they would not be able to switch programs for the five years covered by the farm bill. Farmers with rice and peanut base acres almost all chose the PLC program, while most corn and soybean

36. The minimum price is the reference price under the Price Loss Coverage program; see below.

37. See Ifft and others (2012, p. 5) for figures on direct payments per acre; the Commodity Credit Corporation provides data on payments by program and commodity through the USDA Farm Service Agency website at www.fsa.usda.gov/about-fsa/budget-and-performance-management/budget/ccc-budget-essentials/index.

acreage went into the ARC program. Wheat growers split roughly 50-50.[38] As shown in table 3-2, average peanut and rice prices were near the ARC benchmark price, while corn and soybean prices were well below it.[39] With most commodity prices projected to continue declining, rice and peanuts will benefit more from the downside price risk of PLC. Corn and soybean farmers will generally benefit more from the ARC program, at least for the first few years, because the moving average will likely remain above market prices. This average is likely to change in the last years of the farm bill. Thus, if these projections pan out, and if Congress retains the ARC and PLC programs in the next farm bill in 2019, more farmers are likely to choose the PLC option.[40]

For the 2015 marketing year, USDA's Farm Service Agency reported that, as of early October 2016, payments were $5.6 billion under the ARC program and $1.2 billion under the PLC program.[41] More than half of the total for the two programs, $3.9 billion, was for corn, while payments for soybeans and wheat were just over $1 billion apiece; peanut growers received almost half a billion dollars. Data for payments to rice growers were not available in that report, but had totaled $400 million in 2014. The total for all crops in 2015 was over $7 billion, roughly 40 percent more than what farmers had received in direct and countercyclical payments in each of the last two years of the previous farm bill. As a result of the moving market average, the Congressional Budget Office (CBO) had projected in March 2016 that ARC payments would peak at $6 billion in fiscal year (FY) 2017, and then fall to under $2 billion by FY 2020. By contrast, the CBO projected that PLC payments would rise to around $2.5 billion in each of the fiscal years 2018 to 2020.[42]

The 2014 farm bill's approach to cotton was different because the WTO

---

38. Data on the program elections are available through the USDA Farm Service Agency website at www.fsa.usda.gov/programs-and-services/arcplc_program/index.

39. ARC uses a five-year moving Olympic average to calculate benchmark revenue: they take the prices for the most recent five years, drop the lowest and highest, and calculate the average for the remaining three.

40. Westhoff and others (2016).

41. Data on payments are available on the USDA Farm Service Agency website at www. fsa.usda.gov/programs-and-services/arcplc_program/index; accessed October 18, 2016, when data on payments for the 2015 market year were available up to October 3, 2016.

42. CBO (2016, p. 6).

Table 3-2   Key Price Parameters for New 2014 Farm
Bill Programs, Dollars per Bushel or Pound

Commodity	Fixed reference price	ARC-CO benchmark price, 2014	Market year price, 2014
Corn	3.70	5.29	3.70
Peanuts	0.27	0.28	0.22
Rice			
Long grain	0.14	0.14	0.11
Medium grain	0.14	0.15	0.14
Soybeans	8.40	12.27	10.10
Wheat	5.50	6.60	5.99

Source: From Program Year 2014, data are available from the USDA Farm Service Agency at www.fsa.usda.gov/programs-and-services/arcplc_program/arcplc-program-data/index (accessed May 20, 2016).

had ruled that previous subsidies were in breach of U.S. commitments and reducing those subsidies had been a key target in international trade negotiations. The United States and Brazil had negotiated a temporary settlement of the WTO dispute under which the United States provided compensation to Brazil and made some tweaks to its support for cotton. In an effort to resolve the problem once and for all, the farm bill created a separate revenue insurance program just for cotton that meets one key Brazilian demand: not setting a target price for cotton.[43] With the new STAX program, cotton farmers can guarantee that they will receive up to 90 percent of the average revenue for the area in which they are located (usually the county) and taxpayers will pick up the tab for 80 percent of the insurance premium.

Participation in the STAX program for cotton has been relatively low, however—only 28 percent of (upland) cotton acres were insured under the program—and cotton farmers are lobbying for additional protection

43. See "Industries Reach Deal on WTO Cotton Dispute; May Not Satisfy Brazil," *Inside U.S. Trade,* June 6, 2013.

from low prices.[44] Producers want USDA to add cottonseed, the oil from which is used in fried and other processed food products, to the list of "other oilseeds" that are eligible for the PLC and ARC programs. In recent years, the cottonseed price has been well below the PLC reference price for other oilseeds, and one analysis estimates that payments could reach $1 billion per year under that program.[45] In February 2016, Secretary of Agriculture Tom Vilsack denied the request, saying that Congress would need to authorize it, and find a way to pay for it.[46] In June, however, Vilsack's department announced it would provide one-time payments of up to $40,000 per cotton farmer, $300 million in total, under a program designed to reduce the costs of processing cotton.[47]

Finally, the farm bill affirms that crop insurance will remain a key part of the farm safety net. Market failures are common in insurance markets and it makes sense for public policy to move in the direction of helping farmers manage risk. But the average share of the annual crop insurance premiums paid by farmers has fallen from over 70 percent in the early 1990s to under 40 percent in recent years. Zulauf and Orden examine the arguments for subsidizing crop insurance and conclude that the current levels are well beyond what is needed to compensate for market failures.[48] In addition to the substantial premium subsidy, subsidies to private insurance companies for operating costs and reinsurance averaged nearly

---

44. See Don Shurely, "STAX: A By-the-Numbers Look at Its First Year for Cotton Farmers," *Southeast FarmPress*, December 3, 2015, http://southeastfarmpress.com/cotton/stax-numbers-look-its-first-year-cotton-farmers.

45. Zulauf and others (2016).

46. See Philip Brasher, "Vilsack Denies Cotton Growers' Aid Request, Says Congress Must Act," *Agri-Pulse*, February 3, 2016, www.agri-pulse.com/Vilsack-denies-cotton-growers-aid-request-02032016.asp.

47. Subject to certain limits, the payments under the Cotton Ginning Cost Share Program will be based on 2015 cotton acres and 40 percent of ginning costs in each region. Ginning is the process of separating the cotton fiber from the seeds. See the June 6, 2016, news release from the USDA Farm Service Agency at www.fsa.usda.gov/news-room/news-releases/2016/nr_20160606_rel_0140 (accessed July 13, 2016). Former USDA chief economist Joe Glauber and University of California at Davis professor Daniel Sumner discuss the distortions created by purportedly temporary subsidies that turn out to be anything but temporary (Glauber and Sumner 2016).

48. Zulauf and Orden (2016, pp. 258–63). Barnett, Coble, and Mercier (2016) provide a detailed review and analysis of U.S. government support for crop insurance, as well as alternatives to the current system.

$2 billion per year in 2009–13.[49] All told, the CBO has reported that total government costs for crop insurance in 2015 were nearly $8 billion, and it projected that those costs will rise to $9 billion by 2020, well above the value of the direct payments that the farm bill eliminated.[50]

Whither U.S. Farm Policy?

In recent years, as at other times in the past and in Europe as well, agricultural subsidies have been subject to increased pressure from efforts to cut the federal budget. Ideological opposition to government interventions in agricultural markets from the Tea Party faction of the U.S. Congress is also a factor. Zulauf analyzes how the growing cost and other questions about the rationale for crop insurance subsidies could undermine support for this program.[51] Still, optimism that these forces can win out over the U.S. agriculture lobby should be tempered. High-level former and current USDA officials have noted that being optimistic about fundamental reforms "would be to ignore 85 years of history, for if nothing else, agricultural programs have shown themselves to be remarkably resilient."[52] Indeed, agricultural lobbying groups and their congressional advocates are already calling for a reopening of the farm bill to address what they see as holes in the farm safety net.

Most studies conclude that the program changes in the 2014 farm bill are unlikely to cause the United States to breach its commitments under the Uruguay Round agreement. Nevertheless, the new farm bill runs counter to the direction of reforms adopted in the URAA by replacing the decoupled direct payments with new, only partially decoupled subsidies. A number of these studies conclude that U.S. negotiators would find it difficult to stick with the proposal to further reduce subsidies that they put on the table in the Doha Round in the mid-2000s.[53] This backpedaling may not matter much, since the 2015 WTO ministerial meeting effectively

49. Zulauf and Orden (2016, p. 257).

50. CBO (2016, p. 24).

51. Zulauf (2016).

52. Glauber and Effland (2016, p. 26). Glauber is a former USDA chief economist. At the time of writing, Anne Effland was a senior staff economist in the chief economist's office.

53. Babcock and Paulson (2012, p. 1); Glauber and Westhoff (2015); and Zulauf and Orden (2016, pp. 252–53).

ended the Doha Round, but these events could be costly for U.S. farmers as well as taxpayers if it means that the WTO remains stymied on agriculture and, therefore, that emerging market policies continue to be almost entirely free from multilateral discipline.

U.S. FOOD AID STUCK IN THE PAST

Despite some market-oriented reforms in U.S. farm policy over the years, U.S. food aid remains trapped in a 1950s time warp. The major U.S. food aid program, Food for Peace, originated in the 1950s when the government relied on supply management policies to prop up commodity prices. When prices were low, the U.S. government bought up surpluses and then had to dispose of them, sometimes by donating food overseas or by selling it to developing country governments on concessional terms.

Though farm programs changed and the U.S. government is no longer in the business of holding grain stocks, the Food for Peace program still requires that food aid be bought in the United States and mostly transported (50%) on U.S.-flagged ships. This requirement is not only costly in dollars and days of delay, it is inconsistent with the efforts of the U.S. Feed the Future initiative to help make poor farmers more productive and less poor. Other donors, including Canada and most European governments, have moved to using cash that can be used to purchase food locally, regionally, or wherever it is most cost-effective to do so, which means that limited resources reach more people.

The unnecessary costs and inefficiencies of U.S. in-kind food aid practices are well documented by both U.S. government agencies and outside researchers. One of many studies on the topic by the Government Accountability Office compared local and regional purchases by the UN World Food Program (WFP) to in-kind food aid shipped from the United States. The GAO found that WFP transactions typically saved 14 weeks and cost an average of 34 percent less for shipments to Africa. Examining all destinations, food purchased locally was 25 percent less costly than U.S. in-kind food aid.[54] Another GAO study in 2011 investigated monetization, a practice that involves private voluntary organizations receiving

54. U.S. GAO (2009).

donated U.S. commodities that they then sell in developing countries to raise money for their projects. This study found that the monetized commodity transactions recovered, on average, only 75 percent of total costs under U.S. Agency for International Development (USAID) programs and 60 percent for those overseen by the USDA. The result was that, of $700 million expended by the agencies over the three years studied to buy and donate commodities, only around $500 million ultimately was available for development projects. The analysis also concluded that these agencies did not have adequate mechanisms in place to ensure that selling donated U.S. commodities did not disrupt local markets, as required by law. The GAO found that the agencies sometimes allowed relatively large amounts of food to be sold without rigorous market analysis and without ex post evaluation to assess the market impact.[55]

Other studies have come to similar conclusions, including an independent evaluation of a small local and regional purchase pilot program mandated in the 2008 farm bill, as well as a similar study by Lentz, Passarelli, and Barrett.[56] The independent evaluation found that local or regional purchase generally saved an average of 10 to 14 weeks. They looked at transactions in nine different countries and, not surprisingly, found smaller differences in delivery times for nearby countries (Guatemala) or those on major shipping routes (Bangladesh). However, the delays were longer than the average for many landlocked countries and those not on major shipping routes, such as many of the major food aid recipients in Africa. These two studies also found that using local or regional purchase, cash transfers, or vouchers generally was more cost effective than in-kind U.S. food aid, though the savings varied depending on the type of commodity purchased. The independent evaluation by Management Systems International examined 385 transactions in 18 countries, 191 that used local or regional purchase and 194 that procured food in the United States. The evaluation found that commodity costs were generally lower in the United States, but that the transportation, shipping, and handling costs were large enough that purchasing cereals and pulses (beans and

---

55. U.S. GAO (2011, pp. 31–45).
56. Management Systems International (2012); and Lentz, Passarelli, and Barrett (2013).

peas) locally or regionally cost roughly a third less on average.[57] Lentz, Passarelli, and Barrett analyzed 329 transactions, 144 of which used local or regional purchase. This study found cost savings on cereals of around 50 percent and around a quarter for pulses. Local or regional purchase saved little if anything when vegetable oils or other processed foods were needed.[58] Table 3-3 summarizes the results from these two studies.

Other studies have tried to estimate the total cost to U.S. taxpayers from having to transport at least half of food aid shipments on U.S.-flagged vessels. Bageant, Barrett, and Lentz were able to obtain detailed

Table 3-3   Average Cost Reduction from Local or Regional Purchase Compared to U.S.-Sourced Food Aid

	Average cost reduction (percent)	
Commodity	Management Systems International (2012)[a]	Lentz, Passarelli, and Barrett (2013)[b]
Unprocessed cereals	35	53
Emergency deliveries only	45	n.a.
To Africa only	42	n.a.
Milled cereals	18	n.a.
Pulses	31	24
Vegetable oils	-5	n.a.
Fortified or blended foods (for example, corn-soy blend)	16	n.a.
Processed foods (including vegetable oils, fortified and blended products)	n.a.	−8

Sources: Management Systems International (2012); and Lentz, Passarelli, and Barrett (2013).
n.a. = not available.

a. average based on transactions in 2 countries in Central America, 2 in Asia, and 13 in Africa.
b. average based on transactions in 1 country in Central America, 2 in Asia, and 6 in Africa.

57. Management Systems International (2012).
58. Lentz, Passarelli, and Barrett (2013).

data on food aid shipments in 2006 from USAID. They concluded that the cargo preference requirement raised shipping costs by $140 million, roughly the equivalent of nonemergency aid to Africa that year.[59] Moreover, while national security needs in an emergency provide the rationale for the cargo preference requirements, this study concluded that 70 percent of the ships used did not meet the condition that they should be militarily useful in case of an emergency. In 2015, the GAO found that food aid shipping costs were higher by $107 million in 2011–14 owing to cargo preference.[60] This figure is much lower than that found by Bageant and others, but that is partly because food aid shipments were lower than in 2006 and Congress had lowered the cargo preference requirement from 75 percent to 50 percent.

Thus, the benefits of reform seem clear but the interests supporting the current system—farm organizations, shipping companies, and maritime unions, as well as private voluntary organizations using monetization to raise funds—are well entrenched. In the mid-2000s, they successfully defeated efforts by President George W. Bush's administration to untie 25 percent of the food aid budget. A small, $75 million, five-year pilot project to study the effects of local and regional purchase was as far as Congress was willing to go.[61]

In 2013, President Barack Obama tried again. The administration's FY 2014 budget proposed to eliminate monetization and untie the nonemergency food aid budget, as well as untie 45 percent of emergency food aid. For the untied portion of the budget, the reform would allow USAID to use whatever means best fit a given situation: U.S. sourcing, local and regional purchase, cash transfers, or vouchers. The other half of emergency food aid would remain subject to the in-kind and cargo preference mandates. Overall, USAID estimated that the proposal would allow roughly the same level of funds aid to reach an additional 4 million people. Elliott and McKitterick estimated less conservatively that the number of additional people helped would be at least 4 million to 6 million and possibly as many as 10 million.[62]

---

59. Bageant, Barrett, and Lentz (2010).
60. U.S. GAO (2015, highlights page).
61. See Management Systems International (2012) for details on the farm bill provisions.
62. Elliott and McKitterick (2013). Just as there are concerns about monetization or other

Throughout 2014 and 2015, the chairs of the House and Senate committees overseeing foreign assistance supported food aid reform. In conjunction with Democratic colleagues, they introduced legislation that would have gone further than the administration's proposals and eliminated the requirements for in-kind food aid and monetization. While these efforts have not been successful, it is interesting to note that, during the House debate on the farm bill, an amendment calling for reforms akin to the administration's proposal fell short by just 17 votes (203 for and 220 against). This was a narrower margin than for the farm bill as a whole, which was initially voted down, 195 for and 234 opposed, before finally passing in early 2014.[63]

The continued opposition to food aid reform from narrow special interests is particularly unfortunate now. The United States is still the world's single largest food aid donor, but higher costs mean that the same amount of funding today buys far less than it did a decade ago. At the same time, the crisis in Syria, multiple conflicts in Africa as well as in Afghanistan and Iraq, and more frequent weather shocks mean that many more people are in need of food assistance. In 2015, the WFP was so short of funding that it had to cut its assistance to Syrian refugees in neighboring countries by as much as half.[64]

INTERNATIONAL COOPERATION IN SUPPORT
OF AGRICULTURAL REFORM

The history of agricultural trade negotiations is not promising for those who would like to see stronger constraints on beggar-thy-neighbor policies and reforms to obviously inefficient boondoggles like U.S. food aid. From the beginning, the postwar GATT had looser rules for agriculture than for manufacturing. American negotiators ensured that agriculture

---

in-kind food aid disrupting local markets and suppressing prices for local producers, local purchase could do the opposite if markets are not sufficiently flexible and well integrated. Ensuring that increased flexibility leads to greater effectiveness requires careful evaluation of local market conditions.

63. See Kripke (2013) for an analysis of the votes.

64. See the WFP news release, "WFP Executive Director Implores Global Community to Continue Support for Syrian Refugees," WFP, August 13, 2015, www.wfp.org/news/news-release/wfp-executive-director-implores-global-community-continue-support-syrian-refugee-0.

would remain largely outside the rules when it bowed to congressional pressure in the 1950s and got a waiver to protect key U.S. policies from challenge. They regretted that move almost immediately as U.S. policy began moving to greater export orientation and the original European Economic Community created the highly distortionary CAP in the early 1960s.

The Uruguay Round of trade negotiations, launched by GATT members in Punta del Este in 1986, was the first to seriously try and address the array of trade-distorting agricultural policies.[65] But that 1994 agreement proved to be yet another disappointment. On the positive side, agricultural policies were, for the first time, subject to constraints under international trade rules and levels of support were capped. The caps, however, were generally well above the levels of support that countries were providing. European negotiators ensured that the rules reflected the modest reforms they had already adopted and Japan insisted on keeping tight restrictions on rice and other sensitive imports. American negotiators, though they had strenuously pushed for stronger rules to constrain EU subsidies and open the Japanese and other markets, insisted on retaining protection for American sugar, dairy, and other import-sensitive sectors. Overall, the URAA's constraints were so loose that they had little impact on agricultural policies in practice.

The WTO decided to launch a new round of trade negotiations in Doha in 2001, just as real agricultural prices were slumping to historic lows. Building on the Uruguay Round framework, the goal was to achieve sharp cuts in actual levels of price-depressing agricultural subsidies and trade barriers. This time, however, Brazil and other developing country exporters were also in the forefront demanding reform. U.S. farmers and negotiators, who had been strong proponents of reform in the Uruguay Round, saw the new round as an opportunity to increase market access in fast-growing developing countries. But American subsidy programs also came under uncomfortable scrutiny and, as time wore on, U.S. negotiators showed less interest in giving them up.

---

65. See Elliott (2006; 2015) and the sources cited therein.

The Doha Round Falters

By the time the Doha Round was launched in 2001, tariffs on manufactured goods in high-income countries were mostly in the low single digits, and the tariff peaks that remained were mostly in agriculture. Thus, agriculture was what the richer countries had to give in the round if they wanted to get increased access for other goods and services in developing countries in return. In addition to pressure from agricultural exporters, including Brazil, Chile, Australia, and New Zealand, development advocacy groups also subjected agricultural policies in high-income countries to scathing criticism for contributing to global poverty.

When food prices began to rise, things changed dramatically. The 2007–08 price spikes shifted global attention from the effects of low commodity prices on poor producers to the effect of high food prices on poor consumers, as discussed in the previous chapter. The policy focus shifted from countercyclical price support for farmers in rich countries to subsidies and mandates for biofuels that contributed to spiking food prices—the subject of the next chapter. During this period, many developing country governments tried to insulate consumers from price spikes. According to the UN Food and Agriculture Organization, 25 countries imposed restrictions on food exports in 2007–08; import-dependent countries also lowered tariffs and taxes on food, bolstering global demand. Russian restrictions on wheat exports contributed to a second round of price spikes in 2010. These policies made sense to each country individually, but taken together they drove global food prices even higher and left everyone else worse off. Export restrictions are also a problem for longer-term food security because they reduce incentives to expand production in countries using them.

Yet the Doha Round negotiations in 2008 seemed strangely disconnected from the changing reality. A key ministerial meeting that summer broke down in part because American and Indian negotiators could not resolve a disagreement over how much latitude developing countries should have to *raise* tariffs when prices are *falling* and imports are surging.[66] Export restrictions in agriculture, which have few constraints under

66. Blustein (2008) tells the story of the failed ministerial meeting.

WTO rules, are still not being addressed. At that time and since, India has essentially taken the stance that the WTO should permit developing countries to do pretty much anything in the name of food security, whatever the costs to their own or other countries.

Incrementalism Produces Modest Results

Though some refuse to let it die, the chances for a successful Doha Round effectively ended at that ministerial meeting in July 2008. After several years of the negotiations being effectively moribund, some WTO trade ministers pushed to salvage what they could from the round. At the 2013 ministerial meeting in Bali, WTO members agreed to move forward on a modest and relatively uncontroversial package of trade facilitation measures, mainly reforms aimed at making the customs process more transparent and efficient. In addition, there was a package of relatively modest steps on agriculture and another package of similarly modest, mainly symbolic measures aimed at helping the least developed members.[67]

Yet even these agreements were not easy to secure. Indian negotiators held up the agreement on trade facilitation until members agreed to address concerns that someone might mount a legal challenge to India's public stockholding scheme. The URAA permits the use of public stocks for food security programs, but setting a fixed price for purchases of stocks is potentially trade-distorting and is subject to discipline under WTO rules. India uses such a system, and with the costs increasing sharply, Indian officials saw a legal challenge as a growing risk. WTO members eventually acquiesced to India's demand and agreed on a "peace clause" under which they temporarily would forgo challenges to public stockholding programs in developing countries, even if such programs also incorporate potentially trade-distorting price support for farmers.[68] Members also agreed that they should find a permanent solution for the problem by the time of the 2017 ministerial meeting. The following summer, India blocked the

67. A summary of the Bali outcome is available from the WTO website at www.wto.org/english/news_e/news13_e/mc9sum_07dec13_e.htm.

68. The WTO provides a useful summary of the issues in the agricultural negotiations fact sheet "The Bali Decision on Stockholding for Food Security in Developing Countries," updated November 27, 2014, available at www.wto.org/english/tratop_e/agric_e/factsheet_agng_e.htm; see also Elliott (2015a).

first steps toward implementation of the Trade Facilitation Agreement because it did not think that progress on a permanent solution for its food security concerns was being made fast enough. American and other negotiators eventually agreed to push for a solution by the end of 2015.

While the outcome in Bali was essentially an agreement to further loosen disciplines on agriculture, the 2015 Nairobi ministerial meeting made modest progress in the other direction. The centerpiece was an agreement to abolish agricultural export subsidies. Traditionally, the EU had been the major user of export subsidies, but had already mostly phased them out as part of its CAP reforms. The agreement was nevertheless useful in locking in those reforms, and in getting developing countries to agree to phase out or forgo entirely the use of export subsidies. An attempt to extend disciplines to other export policies that might be disguised export subsidies was watered down due to U.S. unwillingness to change its policies on export finance and food aid. The outcome did not resolve the public stockholding issue but did affirm that the interim arrangement, barring legal challenges, would remain in place until a permanent solution was agreed upon, hopefully by end-2017. Finally, while India and some other developing countries resisted, the Nairobi declaration effectively ended the Doha Round of trade negotiations.

BEYOND DOHA

The agricultural trade agenda is far different today than it was when the Doha Round was launched in 2001. While the old issues linger and still need to be tackled, the WTO also needs to update the agenda to address concerns about food security and other new issues. While a broad agreement on new disciplines for agriculture does not appear to be on the horizon, WTO members should keep pushing for at least incremental progress wherever possible.[69] In the meantime, good government groups, development advocates, and other reform-minded players need to keep pushing their governments to undertake domestic reforms.

In the United States, reform would mean not backtracking on the

---

69. If prospects for a broader agreement improve, Glauber (2016b) offers sensible recommendations for how to move forward in a number of areas.

modest market-oriented features of the 2014 farm bill, reducing crop insurance premium subsidies, reforming the increasingly costly program protecting domestic sugar producers, and bringing food aid policies into the 21st century. In building the case for broader reform, budget pressures can be a powerful ally. With the increase in crop insurance subsidies and countercyclical subsidies going up again in the United States, and with China and India expanding an array of support programs, trade negotiations might again become an attractive way for governments to tie their own hands while also restraining others' levels of support. The Nairobi ministerial decision to eliminate export subsidies will help because it limits governments' ability to shift some of the costs of domestic policies onto the rest of the world.

The WTO's primary role is to help steer countries in the direction of policies that are less trade-distorting and to use negotiations to lock in any reforms that are achieved. As part of these efforts, members should keep pushing to ensure the effective implementation of the Uruguay Round disciplines, especially the requirements to report on domestic policies, and to make incremental progress on some of the issues identified since Nairobi.[70] Members also need a solution on public stockholding programs that does not permanently open a major new loophole for providing producer support.[71] And, while monitoring implementation of the new commitments on export competition, the United States will remain under pressure to reform food aid and reduce the subsidy element of its agricultural export credit programs. Modest steps providing for transparency and consultations with affected members before using export restrictions in the midst of food price spikes could be another part of the short-run, incremental agenda.

To succeed with something larger, WTO members will need to find new ways to approach trade negotiations. Both the Uruguay and Doha rounds were launched as "single undertakings," meaning that nothing

70. See the March 8, 2016, news item from the WTO agriculture negotiations at www.wto.org/english/news_e/news16_e/agng_09mar16_e.htm; see also the summary of the chair's report from a May 9 meeting at www.wto.org/english/news_e/news16_e/agng_13may16_e.htm (both accessed June 6, 2016).

71. Elliott (2015a) offers one potential fix while Glauber (2016a) provides an excellent analysis of the overall problem and a range of possible solutions.

was agreed unless everything was agreed—agriculture, nonagricultural market access, services, and everything else. While the Uruguay Round produced an agreement under this approach, it may have been a pyrrhic victory. Many developing countries felt that they got less on market access for agriculture and labor-intensive manufactures than they gave on intellectual property and other new rules. These countries' demands for some "rebalancing" were a major contributor to the Doha Round's unraveling. Thus, the single undertaking model for trade negotiations has now clearly failed, and the Doha Round along with it. With agricultural support programs spreading, including into large emerging markets, there would seem to be more than enough costly and trade-distorting policies in place to provide bargaining chits for a deal just within agriculture. An incremental approach will be slower and less ambitious than many would hope, but it is better than no progress at all.

Agricultural policy reform must remain on the development agenda because trade is a key tool to alleviate poverty and to bring food security to an estimated 800 million people around the world who remain chronically undernourished. Better policies to make agriculture in developing countries more productive and profitable, including via exports, would help achieve both these goals. Stronger international trade rules would help by constraining the beggar-thy-neighbor policies that distort trade, contribute to price volatility, reduce confidence in global markets, and discourage investments in developing country agriculture. American farmers that rely on export markets would also benefit from more effective disciplines on agricultural subsidies and trade barriers. Agriculture may not be new on the trade agenda, or as sexy as e-commerce, but it is still important.

4

BIOFUEL POLICIES AT THE EXPENSE OF
FOOD SECURITY AND CLIMATE CHANGE

ALTHOUGH U.S. BIOFUEL SUPPORT POLICIES are nominally aimed at enhancing energy security and mitigating climate change, they have been more effective at propping up prices for corn and soybean farmers and demand for biofuel producers. Indeed, at times, such as in the 1990s, bolstering demand for agricultural commodities moved to the fore as a motivation for U.S. and European Union policies. While there is a debate about the degree to which biofuel *policies* contributed to the food price spikes of 2007–08, there is little question that the sharp and sudden increase in biofuel demand played an important role.

At the same time that concerns about potential conflicts between biofuels and food security were growing, scientific and economic research undercut the assumption that first-generation biofuels have been contributing to climate change mitigation. We have long known that the amount by which biofuels reduce greenhouse gas emissions, relative to fossil fuels, varies widely and depends on how the crops are grown and processed. Recent research that directly measures all emissions across specific biofuel supply chains shows that corn ethanol, under typical U.S. operating conditions, can result in higher levels of net emissions than fossil fuels. Cutting forests or plowing virgin lands to grow feedstocks, or to grow food to replace the crops now going into fuel, generates additional GHG emissions that further undermine the case in favor of first-generation biofuels.

Any talk of biofuel policy reform faces stiff opposition from U.S. and EU farmers, who reap higher incomes from the increased demand for their crops, and from biofuel refiners, which would be smaller and fewer in number without government support. Yet the calls for reform were loud enough in Europe to contribute to a modest rollback of the consumption mandate there. In the United States, a rising chorus of complaints is coming from some strange bedfellows—antihunger advocates and environmentalists concerned about the global impact of biofuels, along with the livestock industry and big oil companies and refiners concerned about their own bottom lines. Because of this growing opposition, along with mounting technical obstacles to implementation, the moment may now be ripe for reform of U.S. biofuel policy as well.

BIOFUEL POLICIES AND FOOD PRICES

With agricultural commodity prices at historic lows around the turn of the millennium, subsidies to promote biofuel use seemed like a solution for multiple problems (see chapter 2, figure 2-1). Replacing petroleum-based fuels with ethanol or biodiesel made from corn, wheat, sugar, or oilseeds would prop up prices for struggling farmers. In theory, it would also reduce GHG emissions and promote energy independence. While the weight attached to these rationales differed across countries and over time, numerous countries, led by the United States and the EU, embraced policies to accelerate biofuel development.[1]

Shortly after, everything began to change. Commodity prices started rising and then spiked sharply (figure 4-1). As described in chapter 2, the impact of higher food prices on the poor in developing countries is mixed, but surging prices (such as in 2007–08) and the increased volatility that often follows are not helpful to anyone. Chapter 2 briefly discussed vari-

---

1. For another assessment of biofuels policies and how they are performing against these goals, see Gerasimchuk and others (2012); on the political economy of agricultural support as a motivation, see Naylor (2012, p. 5).

ous factors that have contributed to the price spikes and increased food price volatility in the late 2000s. This section looks more closely at the rising demand for biofuels and the role that biofuel policies may have played in such food price increases and subsequent volatility.

Trends in Biofuel Demand

Figure 4-1 shows the steep rise in biofuel consumption from 2000 to 2008 and beyond, and how closely correlated it was with rapidly rising energy and food prices. In 2000, biofuel consumption was 20 billion liters worldwide, less than 2 percent of global gasoline sales, and almost all of it was in Brazil and the United States. Just over a decade later, thanks in part to increased subsidies and government mandates, biofuel consumption was five times larger and the EU had emerged as the third-largest market (figure 4-2). Roughly two-thirds of the balance is in Argentina, Canada, China, India, Indonesia, and Thailand.

Brazil began encouraging the production and consumption of sugarcane-based ethanol as an alternative fuel after the oil price spikes of the 1970s and early 1980s.[2] The United States introduced modest subsidies for ethanol at the same time, but consumption remained trivial until a convergence of policy and market changes led to a sharp increase in the early 2000s. U.S. consumption now accounts for almost half the world's total, while EU consumption, which barely registered in 2000, caught up with Brazil before flattening out. As this chapter will discuss, U.S. ethanol consumption is also flattening, in part because of technical obstacles to blending higher shares of ethanol in gasoline.

Although these three markets still account for 70 percent of total global consumption, consumption elsewhere has been growing and other countries have introduced biofuel mandates in recent years. According to the 2014 *Global Sustainability Report*, the number of countries with biofuel support policies increased from 10 in 2005 to 66 in 2015.[3] Many of the developing countries that adopted policies to support biofuel use became more cautious after commodity prices surged in 2007–08, however. Few of the blending mandates, which generally fall in the 2 percent to 10 per-

2. Valdes (2011) discusses the current status of policy and production in Brazil.

3. REN21 (2016, p. 19).

Figure 4-1   Trends in Commodity Prices and Biofuels Consumption, 2000–14

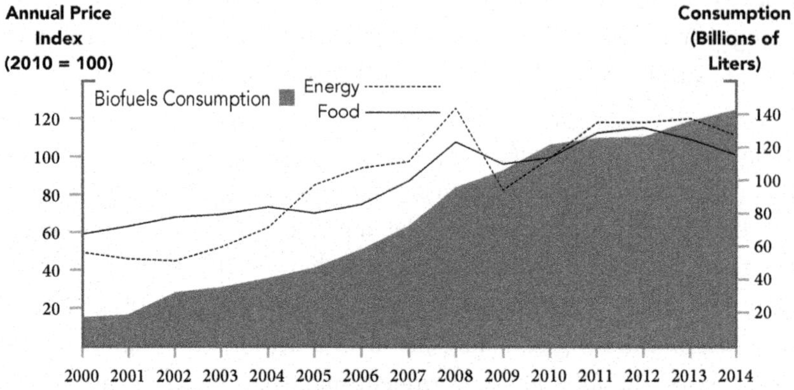

Sources: Prices: World Bank Commodity Price Data (accessed October 2016); Biofuels consumption: OECD-FAO Agricultural Outlook.

cent range, are being met.[4] Moreover, annual new investments in biofuels peaked at $29 billion in 2007 and fell to just $4.9 billion in 2013.[5]

Two worrisome exceptions to this story are Indonesia and Argentina. These countries had been producing biodiesel mainly for export to the European market. After the EU blocked their exports to protect the domestic biofuel industry, both countries ramped up their mandates for domestic consumption to absorb the lost exports and support feedstock prices. Argentina and Indonesia use soybean oil and palm oil, respectively, as feedstocks for biodiesel. From a climate change perspective, these biofuel choices are worrisome because those commodities are two of four identified as particular concerns for their potential contribution to deforestation.[6]

Biofuels and Food Price Volatility

Although environmentalists hope that biofuels can one day be made at commercial scale from algae, crop residues, other waste, or perennial grasses and shrubs grown on marginal lands unsuitable for food crops,

4. IEA (2011, pp. 10–12); and Timilsina and Shrestha (2010, pp. 6–8, 12).

5. REN21 (2014, p. 15).

6. Persson, Henders, and Kastner (2014).

Figure 4-2   Trends in Biofuels Consumption in Selected Countries, 2000–14

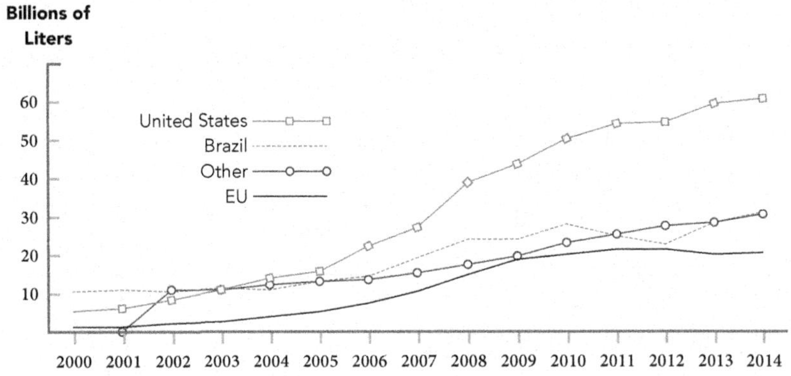

Billions of Liters

Source: OECD-FAO Agricultural Outlook.

Notes: Other countries include biodiesel in Brazil, Argentina, and Indonesia, and ethanol in China, India, and Thailand.

the vision remains an elusive one. In the meantime, biofuels divert relatively large amounts of food crops to fuel: corn and soybeans in the United States; rapeseed and sugar beets in Europe (table 4-1).

As figure 4-1 shows, the correlation between rising biofuel demand and rising food prices is clear. The causal links, though, are complicated and there continues to be a debate over the relative contribution of biofuel demand to the 2007–08 food price spikes. There is an even more intense debate over the role of biofuel support *policies* in stimulating the growth in demand. Some researchers attribute the price spikes to a number of factors converging in a "perfect storm" in the mid-2000s. Many agree that increased biofuel demand played a role, but conclude that the spikes were driven primarily by closer market links between food and oil prices that had little to do with policy. Others have concluded that biofuel policies were the most important factor in the price spikes and the subsequent volatility.[7]

7. For a review of the early literature, see Elliott (2008). The second issue of the 2013 volume of the journal *Global Food Security* includes articles by a number of key participants in the debate that update the story and further analyze the links between biofuels and food prices. De Gorter, Drabik, and Just (2015) is a comprehensive review of biofuel policies in the big three markets and provides a detailed analysis of the economics of biofuels that

Table 4-1   Transportation Fuels and Feedstocks in the
United States and European Union, 2014

	United States	European Union
Gasoline		
Share of road transportation fuels	75	28
Ethanol share of gasoline	10	4
Major feedstocks (percent)	corn: 95	corn: 25 sugar beet: 53
Diesel		
Share of road transportation fuels	25	72
Biodiesel share of diesel	3.2	5.3
Major feedstocks (percent)	soybean oil: 46 canola, corn oils: 19 recycled oils: 12	rapeseed oil: 55 recycled oils: 14 palm oil: 14

Sources: U.S. Department of Energy, *Monthly Energy Review*, September 2016, tables
3.7c, 10.3, and 10.4; Schnepf (2013, p. 2); U.S. Energy Information Administration, *Monthly
Biodiesel Production Report*, July 2016, Table 3; Flach and others (2015, pp. 12–13, and 22).

Higher oil prices contribute directly to higher food prices by raising
costs for farm machinery use, fertilizer (which is energy-intensive to produce), and transportation. They also contribute indirectly by increasing
demand for biofuels, which increases demand for feedstock crops. The
link between increased demand for biofuel feedstocks and rising prices
for those crops—mainly coarse grains and vegetable oils—is clear. Given
that the United States is such a large player in both corn and ethanol markets, it is not surprising that most analysts point to the increase in ethanol
production as the major cause of rising corn prices from 2005 to the peak
in 2008.[8]

In a survey of some 20 studies conducted between 2008 and 2013, cov-
ering more than 100 scenarios, Condon and others note the wide variation in estimates of the impact of biofuels on corn prices. They control

---

concludes the impact of biofuels policy on food prices was significant.

8. Yacobucci and Schnepf (2007); Collins (2008); Rosegrant (2008); and de Gorter, Drabik,
and Just (2013).

for differences across the studies that might account for the variation and find, on average, that the estimated impact on corn prices was 2 percent to 3 percent for each 1 billion gallons of additional ethanol production in the long run. Not surprisingly, the impact was larger in the short run, averaging 5 percent to 10 percent. This analysis suggests that the increase in U.S. ethanol production from 2006 to 2008 of around 4 billion gallons could have been responsible for a sizable chunk of the increase in corn prices over that period.[9]

The links between ethanol, corn, and other crop prices are harder to pin down. Wheat prices rose in part because some livestock producers chose to substitute it for relatively more expensive feed corn in their operations. Drought in key growing areas in this period also contributed to rising wheat prices. Government actions also played an important role, especially in rice markets. With global grain prices rising, and a poor wheat harvest suppressing domestic food supplies, India banned wheat exports in early 2007 and rice exports later that year. As the increases in food prices began accelerating, other developing countries took similar action to restrict rice exports and the Philippines began placing large orders to import rice. Thus, the 2008 spike in rice prices had little to do with fundamentals and was primarily the result of panicked hoarding.[10] Some trace the panic in developing countries back to the biofuels policy; others treat it as a separate phenomenon.

Abbott, Hurt, and Tyner (in 2008) and Baffes (in 2013) identify a range of earlier trends that set the stage for the price spikes, including strong economic growth, particularly in the emerging markets; a long period of declining investments in crop yields; the depreciating dollar; and increasing demand from investment funds to add commodities to their portfolios. With this as background, short-run influences—rising energy prices, low grain stocks, weather shocks in key grain-producing areas, and biofuels growth—triggered the price spikes.[11] Tyner, summarizing a series of articles coauthored with Philip Abbott and Christopher Hurt, concludes

9. Condon, Klemick, and Wolverton (2013, p. 4).

10. Slayton (2009); Dawe and Slayton (2010); and de Gorter, Drabik, and Just (2013, pp. 85–86).

11. Abbott, Hurt, and Tyner (2008); and Baffes (2013).

that it is impossible to disentangle the effects of biofuels from these other factors.[12]

In addition to the debate over the relative role that increasing biofuels demand had on food prices, there is also a debate over the role that biofuel policies played. For example, Tyner reports earlier estimates that $3 of the increased corn price was due to higher oil prices and only $1 to the U.S. subsidies that were in place at the time.[13] Babcock notes that the U.S. ethanol mandate was not binding in 2007–08, and that only the U.S. tax credit for blending ethanol with gasoline (see below) could have had any impact. He estimates that corn prices, which doubled from 2005–06 to 2007–08, would have been just 7 percent lower if the subsidies had not been in place.[14]

Among those attributing a larger role in the price spikes to biofuels early on was World Bank economist Donald Mitchell, who estimated that "three-quarters of the 140 percent actual [food price] increase [from 2002 to 2008] was due to biofuels and the related consequences of low grain stocks, large land use shifts, speculative activity, and export bans."[15] A more recent analysis that focuses on the role of market fundamentals comes to a similar conclusion, finding that, *against a backdrop of tighter commodity markets,* "biofuels policy was the major driver of the price spikes."[16] In a major new book on the economics of biofuels and biofuels policy, de Gorter, Drabik, and Just conclude that "biofuel policies made, by far, the greatest contribution to food commodity price levels and volatility" and that "there would be no biofuels without policies."[17]

There is no question that high gasoline prices would have generated rising demand for ethanol in the mid-2000s, even without U.S. subsidies. And figure 4-3 (p. 86) shows the degree to which actual corn ethanol consumption exceeded the mandate at the time of the price spikes in 2007–08. But stopping the analysis there ignores the role played by decades of subsidies, and the Clean Air Act regulations that generated demand for

12. Tyner (2013).
13. Ibid., p. 128.
14. Babcock (2011, p. 6).
15. Mitchell (2008, p. 1).
16. Wright (2014, p. 88).
17. De Gorter, Drabik, and Just (2015, p. 3).

ethanol as a gasoline additive (details below). Those government policies helped create the biofuel industry in the first place.

Commodity prices are falling now, partly because of slower growth in China and Europe and partly because the old saw about higher prices being their own best antidote remains true in the short run.[18] But over the longer run, the underlying demand pressures on food prices will not abate any time soon and it remains to be seen whether the supply side can continue to keep up. Yield growth has been slowing for decades, and U.S. investment in research and development to reverse the trend has been slowing as well.

Increasingly frequent severe weather events as a result of climate change are not going to help. Moreover, Searchinger and Heimlich argue that growing demand for agriculture and forestry products creates a competition for land that could further exacerbate climate change:

> The world needs to close a 70 percent gap between the crop calories that were available in 2006 and the calorie needs anticipated in 2050. During the same period, demand for meat and dairy [which consume lots of grain as feed] is projected to grow by more than 80 percent, and demand for commercial timber and pulp is likely to increase by roughly the same percentage. Yet three-quarters of the world's land area capable of supporting vegetation is already managed or harvested to meet human food and fiber needs. Much of the rest contains the world's remaining natural ecosystems, which need to be conserved and restored to store carbon and combat climate change, to protect freshwater resources, and to preserve the planet's biological diversity.[19]

In sum, biofuel policies contributed to creating a relatively large, new, and inelastic source of demand for food crops at a time when commodity prices were either rising or poised to do so. Rising oil prices separately

---

18. FAO Food Price Index data are available on the FAO website at www.fao.org/worldfoodsituation/foodpricesindex/en/.

19. Searchinger and Heimlich (2015, p. 1). On the importance and cost effectiveness of preserving and restoring tropical forests, see Seymour and Busch (2016).

increased the demand for biofuels, but, as argued by de Gorter, Drabik, and Just, there would not have been a biofuel industry in a position to respond without government subsidies.[20] And with the oil price collapse in 2015–16, mandates are now playing a bigger role in propping up biofuel demand. While the pressure on food security may be less than when prices were spiking, the possibility that biofuels are aggravating rather than mitigating climate change remains a major concern.

BIOFUELS AND CLIMATE CHANGE

When policymakers began ramping up support for biofuel policies in the 2000s, there was broad support for replacing gasoline and diesel with renewable fuels as part of a policy to address climate change. The transportation sector is responsible for 14 percent of global GHG emissions, more than two-thirds of which are from road transport, and there are few alternatives to biofuels to replace fossil fuels in the short run.[21] A growing body of research, however, is raising questions about the benefits of first-generation biofuels in mitigating climate change. Some current biofuels may even result in higher net GHG emissions than regular gasoline or diesel.

An early strand of research focused on the economic and energy efficiency with which current food-based feedstocks are transformed into fuel. These studies often use "life cycle analysis," which purports to track emissions from the field to the tailpipe, to compare emissions from biofuels to those from fossil fuels. In these studies, net emissions vary widely and depend on how producers grow feedstock crops—how much fertilizer they use, for example—and how plants process the feedstocks, including whether the facility uses coal, natural gas, or biomass for power.[22] The source of the biofuel feedstocks and the degree to which they lead to land use changes that release stored carbon also matter in these analyses.

Other recent research argues that life cycle analyses incorrectly assume

20. De Gorter, Drabik, and Just (2015).

21. IPCC (2014a; 2014b).

22. The Gallagher Review (Renewable Fuels Agency 2008, p. 23) illustrates this analysis for ethanol from wheat, depending only on the processing technology used.

that biofuels are carbon neutral—that is, that the carbon absorbed by the crop during growth offsets the carbon emitted when the fuel is burned. That assumption, it is suggested, amounts to double counting, since the land used for biofuel feedstocks probably was already being used for food production and was sequestering carbon during growth. Directly measuring emissions at each stage of the supply chain, without the assumption of carbon neutrality, changes the results of biofuel emissions studies dramatically.[23]

Taken together, this growing body of research strongly supports the conclusion that most food-based biofuels are doing little if anything to reduce GHG emissions. Many policymakers nevertheless say that they support the current generation of biofuels as a bridge to new cellulosic or other biofuel technologies that will both be more efficient and avoid pressures to cultivate new land. But there is no evidence that support for the first-generation biofuels is contributing to development of more advanced biofuels. Moreover, there are a growing number of questions about how much the biofuel technologies on the horizon can realistically help mitigate climate change.[24]

Not All Biofuels Are the Same

Whatever method one uses to assess them, the economic efficiency and environmental efficacy of different biofuel feedstocks and production processes vary widely. As a result, the estimates of potential reductions in GHG emissions from replacing fossil fuels with the currently available biofuels also vary widely (table 4-2). To take an extreme case, when ethanol is made from corn that is grown with copious amounts of energy-intensive fertilizer; cultivated, harvested, and transported with fossil fuel–burning vehicles; and processed in a coal-powered plant, the resulting fuel likely will emit more greenhouse gases over its life cycle than regular gasoline would.[25] At the other end, recycled vegetable oil, for example from fast-food restaurant fryers, is generally the most efficient and environmentally friendly, but supplies are limited.

Of those biofuels that do not use recycled material as feedstocks, most

23. DeCicco and Krishnan (2015); and Searchinger and Heimlich (2015).

24. Searchinger and Heimlich (2015).

25. Yacobucci and Bracmort (2010, pp. 7–9).

Table 4-2   Reduction in Greenhouse Gas Emissions
Relative to Petroleum-Based Fuels (Percent)

Feedstock	Approximate IEA range (without ILUC)[a]	EU analysis (without ILUC)[b]		U.S. EPA analysis (with ILUC)
		"Typical"	Default	
Waste oil biodiesel	N/A	88	83	86
Rapeseed biodiesel	10 to 80	45	38	n.a.
Soybean biodiesel	N/A	40	31	57
Sugar beet ethanol	30 to 60	61	52	n.a.
Sugarcane ethanol	70 to > 100	71	71	61
Corn ethanol	−20 to 60	56	49	21

Sources: International Energy Agency (2011, p. 16); Flach and others (2011, p. 8); and Yacobucci and Bracmort (2010, p. 18).

n.a. = not applicable; ILUC = indirect land use change.

a. Based on review of 60 life cycle analysis studies.

b. Estimates of the typical reduction in GHG emissions relative to petroleum-based fuels, based on a literature review, are discounted to get the default value for determining each fuel type's eligibility under the EU mandate. Fuels above the mandate's threshold value of 35 percent are eligible; for those below the threshold, producers must submit data showing that their process results in GHG emission savings above 35 percent.

studies find that sugarcane ethanol produced in Brazil reduces net emissions relative to gasoline by around 80 percent.[26] Sugarcane is a relatively high-yield feedstock, so it requires less land and other resources to produce a unit of fuel than many other feedstocks, and Brazil is an efficient sugarcane producer. Processing mills can also use the bagasse (plant residue) to produce heat and power, and some are able to sell electricity to the grid. As long as the ethanol demand does not lead to deforestation

26. The OECD (2008, pp. 47–49) also summarizes a number of these studies. The Gallagher Review (Renewable Fuels Agency 2008, p. 24) does show estimated net negative emissions from a sugarcane ethanol plant in South Africa that uses coal-based electricity from the grid.

or other land use change, Brazil can claim to be contributing to climate change mitigation with its policies promoting sugarcane ethanol.[27]

Other first-generation feedstocks and processes are generally more costly and produce more variable and usually lower net GHG emissions savings. With respect to biodiesel, the recent IPCC report, for example, finds that palm oil is a lower-cost source of biodiesel feedstock because, like sugarcane, it has very high yields of product per unit of land.[28] And, as long as the mill captures the methane produced during processing *and* there is no land use change, the calculated net emissions savings are relatively high. Emissions associated with land use can alter the results of these calculations dramatically, however, as this chapter will discuss.

Nevertheless, all of the calculations using life cycle analysis depend on a key assumption. As described in DeCicco and Krishnan:

> [A]ccounting conventions adopted to date for public policy treat biofuels as inherently carbon neutral, meaning that carbon dioxide (CO_2) from their combustion does not have to be counted because it is offset by CO_2 uptake during feedstock growth. Thus, the prevailing wisdom has been that GHG accounting protocols only need to evaluate production-related emissions.[29]

In effect, this approach assumes that CO_2 uptake was zero before the feedstock was harvested for producing biofuel. Searchinger and Heimlich call this assumption double counting and, like DeCicco and Krishnan they argue that the life cycle approach underestimates the emissions associated with biofuels because it uses the wrong counterfactual.[30]

Since most biofuel feedstocks in the United States (and elsewhere) are grown on productive cropland that otherwise would be used to produce food or livestock feed, the correct counterfactual for measuring the net emissions from biofuels is the difference between the CO_2 uptake from growing food or feed crops versus using the same land to grow biofuel

---

27. IPCC (2014b, pp. 234 and 244).

28. Ibid., p. 245.

29. DeCicco and Krishnan (2015, p. 1).

30. Searchinger and Heimlich (2015, appendixes A and B).

feedstocks. DeCicco and Krishnan use an alternative approach called "annual basis carbon accounting" that explicitly estimates carbon uptake and all the emissions that can be traced directly to the biofuel supply chain. This approach provides an upper-bound estimate of potential emissions savings from biofuels because it ignores potential emissions from indirect land use change. The authors apply their approach to data available for a corn ethanol plant in the United States where a life cycle analysis had been done previously.[31] Without the assumption of carbon neutrality, they find that net emissions across the ethanol supply chain for this facility would be 4 percent higher than using gasoline and shipping the corn and soybeans out for food. Though the authors note that the results are not directly comparable, the earlier life cycle analysis for the same facility estimated that it would reduce net CO_2 emissions by 40 percent compared to gasoline. Moreover, this particular example involved some increased CO_2 uptake that could be attributed to biofuels because farmers switched from growing lower-yielding soybeans to growing only corn, which is higher yielding. In a situation where farmers are already growing corn and simply switch from supplying the food market to supplying the biofuel market, the net emissions from ethanol would be even higher.[32]

Land Use Change Undermines Biofuel Benefits

Another problem with biofuels is that the increased demand for feedstocks, and the associated working through of higher prices in global commodity markets, creates pressures to convert forests and other virgin lands to cropland. This deforestation and virgin land cultivation, in turn, increases GHG emissions and undermines the purported value of biofuels as part of a climate change mitigation strategy. The land use change can be direct, such as if palm oil plantations replace high-carbon peatlands to supply the Indonesian biodiesel industry. Indirect land use change will also result unless crop yields rise fast enough to replace the food now going into fuel tanks without cultivation of new lands. In a Center for Global Development working paper, Busch and Ferretti-Gallon reviewed

---

31. The authors report that the facility uses natural gas and a technology similar to many recently built plants; thus it is not one of those at the extreme end of low net benefits because of coal use or outdated technology.

32. DeCicco and Krishnan (2015, p. 4).

117 studies of the drivers of deforestation and found, not surprisingly, that forest-clearing increases when economic returns on agriculture rise. Higher agricultural prices were more likely to be associated with increased deforestation than nineteen other commonly studied drivers.[33]

In early 2008, *Science* magazine published a series of articles estimating the impact of land use change on assessments of the environmental benefits of biofuels.[34] Fargione and others reported estimates of the number of years that it would take to repay the carbon debts that would be created if various types of native ecosystems were converted to biofuel feedstock production. For palm oil, if biodiesel feedstock producers were to convert either former tropical rainforests or peatlands to plantations, the authors estimated that it would take nearly a century in the former case and more than four centuries in the latter case before biofuel use would make up for the carbon released through deforestation and peatland destruction.[35] Searchinger and others focused on indirect land use changes associated with U.S. corn ethanol consumption, and found that the change in net GHG emissions relative to gasoline shifts from a 20 percent reduction to 93 percent increase if farmers convert virgin land.[36]

A later report prepared for the Intergovernmental Panel on Climate Change (IPCC), using higher-resolution models, found generally lower but still large carbon debts from clearing tropical forests to expand the supply of biofuel feedstocks.[37] Even with higher crop yields, and depending on the crop, if feedstock production results in tropical deforestation it will often take 50 years or more of emissions avoided from not using fossil fuels to make up for the initial carbon release. When producers drain peatlands to put in palm oil plantations, the payback period could be 600 to 900 years.[38]

---

33. Busch and Ferretti-Gallon (2014a); and Busch and Ferretti-Gallon (2014b, p. 3).

34. Examining a range of potential environmental effects, including biodiversity loss and emissions other than CO_2, Scharlemann and Laurance (2008) also found that many first-generation biofuels did not fare well when compared to gasoline.

35. Fargione and others (2008).

36. Searchinger and others (2008).

37. See Chum and others (2011, p. 305); see also Achten and Verchot (2011) for another set of estimates that also show long repayment periods for biodiesel from palm oil, soybean oil, and jatropha under a variety of scenarios.

38. Chum and others (2011, p. 264).

It should be noted, however, that first-generation biofuels from food crops were never really expected to be a big part of the answer to climate change. Rather, they were supposed to be a bridge to more advanced biofuels that would not compete with food for feedstocks and would reduce GHG emissions far more dramatically. Cellulosic and other second-generation biofuel producers are trying to develop products using plant waste, such as corn stalks, or nonfood crops, such as switchgrass or jatropha, that can grow on marginal lands with little alternative use. Algae is a potential third-generation feedstock. But second-generation biofuel technologies are proving more difficult and expensive to develop than anticipated. Moreover, crop residues often have other uses, such as ground cover to maintain soil quality or as livestock fodder. The costs associated with collecting and transporting crop residues to processing plants also raise questions about the economic viability of cellulosic fuels. One recent study suggested that removing corn residue in the American Midwest reduces soil carbon.[39] The authors of this study conclude that incorporating the resulting CO_2 emissions would mean that cellulosic ethanol from this source would not meet the U.S. standard for advanced biofuels.

Assuming that the technological and other obstacles can be overcome, a 2011 IPCC report on bioenergy sees a role for certain types of biofuels as part of climate change mitigation strategies, but only under stringent conditions. The report concludes that growing perennial crops for feedstocks, such as switchgrass, on marginal or degraded lands would contribute the most to climate change mitigation.[40] Yet there are still questions as to whether crops grown on marginal lands will have high enough yields to be profitable. If they are profitable on marginal lands, for that matter, they might be even more profitable on more productive land, which may make it difficult to confine production to marginal areas.

Some researchers see economic as well as climate change mitigation opportunities from the development of biofuels in developing countries, but there are caveats here as well. Schoneveld identifies land that is both suitable for producing biofuel feedstocks and potentially "available," meaning that it is not already forested or under cultivation. He notes,

39. Liska and others (2014).
40. Chum and others (2011).

however, that the land so identified may "not be the most convenient or economically appropriate lands for producers, either because it is not near key transportation routes or markets, or because forested land is less populated." Moreover, local people often use land that is deemed "available" by this relatively broad definition for fuelwood, grazing, or nontimber forest products. Here again, Schoneveld concludes that it would be difficult to ensure that the promotion of biofuels leads to production only on marginal lands that do not threaten food security or increase GHG emissions.[41] Searchinger and Heimlich discuss in detail the difficulties in finding "additional"—that is, currently unused—biomass to use for biofuels.[42]

In sum, the IPCC bioenergy report's conclusion on the conditions needed for sustainable expansion of biomass for energy (including biofuels) suggests caution:

> In order to achieve the high potential deployment levels of biomass for energy, increases in competing food and fibre demand must be moderate, land must be properly managed and agricultural and forestry yields must increase substantially. Expansion of bioenergy *in the absence of monitoring and good governance of land use* carries the risk of significant conflicts with respect to food supplies, water resources and biodiversity, as well as a risk of low GHG benefits.[43]

U.S. BIOFUEL POLICIES

The United States, like Brazil, initially introduced ethanol subsidies in response to the 1970s oil price shocks. Whereas Brazil remained committed to biofuel development, American interest in biofuel subsidies faded along with falling oil prices in the 1980s.[44] U.S. interest revived in the late 1990s as agricultural prices dropped to historic lows (see chapter 2, figure 2-1). Oil prices were also low then, so energy security was not a particular

41. Schoneveld (2010, pp. 6–8).
42. Searchinger and Heimlich (2015).
43. Chum and others (2011, p. 306) (emphasis added).
44. Condon and others (2013, p. 7) provide a timeline of U.S. policies related to biofuels.

concern; neither was reducing GHG emissions a prominent motive. Supporting farm incomes was also a key rationale when the EU replaced some agricultural subsidies for oilseeds with incentives for biodiesel production earlier in the decade (box 4-1).

The initial biofuel subsidy that the U.S. government adopted in the 1970s was a tax credit for blending ethanol with gasoline. The value of the credit varied over the years between $0.40 and $0.60 per gallon. The subsidy spurred some production, but ethanol's share of the U.S. gasoline market was still just 1 percent 20 years later.[45] In the late 1990s, then-President Bill Clinton authorized the U.S. Department of Agriculture to provide modest payments to biofuel producers to increase demand for corn and soybeans. The 2002 farm bill codified those subsidies and added other renewable energy incentives, as did subsequent farm bills.

The next stimulus to ethanol demand was environmental, but it was about air quality, not climate change. The Clean Air Act required refiners to use fuel additives to help engines run more smoothly on unleaded gasoline. Ethanol got a boost after 2003 when California and New York began to phase out the most common additive at the time (methyl tertiary butyl ether) because it was suspected of contaminating groundwater. Refiners turned to ethanol as the least expensive replacement. Then Congress passed the Energy Policy Act of 2005 to ensure "secure, affordable, and reliable energy" through measures aimed at increasing the use of renewable energy sources. This legislation included the first Renewable Fuel Standard (RFS1), and created a mandate for the blending of biofuels in gasoline and diesel.

The RFS1 mandate started at 4 billion gallons in 2006, rising to 7.5 billion gallons by 2012. Rapidly rising gasoline prices, refinery disruptions associated with Hurricane Katrina in late August 2005, and the preexisting tax credit for blending ethanol with gasoline caused a larger-than-expected surge in demand. Ethanol consumption surpassed the mandated blend levels, and Congress responded with the U.S. Energy Independence and Security Act of 2007 (EISA). The revised Renewable Fuel Standard

---

45. The Renewable Fuel Association reports figures on ethanol production, while the Energy Information Administration tracks gasoline consumption. Yacobucci (2012a) details the various federal government incentives for biofuels over the years, as well as those offered by states and local governments.

Box 4-1   EU Biodiesel Subsidies as Farm Support

EU SUPPORT FOR BIOFUELS grew out of its early 1990s Common Agricultural Policy reforms and was shaped by a trade dispute with the United States over oilseed subsidies. By the early 1990s, EU oilseed production had increased tenfold and the value of U.S. soybean exports had been halved, thanks to European subsidies. After an adverse decision under international trade rules and a U.S. threat to impose trade sanctions, the EU agreed to reduce those subsidies. The CAP reform allowed farmers to take land that had been withdrawn from production to boost crop prices and use it to grow industrial crops, including oilseeds for biodiesel. U.S. negotiators wanted to limit the amount of meal, a byproduct of extracting the oil, that could be used for animal feed and thus compete with U.S. soybean exports. To boost demand for the rapeseed oil grown on set-aside land, France and Germany opted to subsidize biodiesel.[a]

In 2003, the European Council adopted a more far-reaching directive and added a biofuels blend target of 2 percent of transportation fuels in 2005 rising to 5.75 percent by 2010.[b] This time around, the directive justified the policy as necessary to comply with the EU's Kyoto Protocol commitments to reduce greenhouse gas emissions, but it also touted benefits in terms of energy security and the opening of new markets for "innovative agricultural products."[c] In 2009, even though food prices were recovering from the impact of the Great Recession, the Commission adopted the Renewable Energy Directive (RED). This directive raised the biofuel blend target to 10 percent of transportation fuels by 2020.

a. Iceland (1994); and USDA (2013).
b. EU (2003).The EU's policy to encourage the use of renewable energy for electricity generation includes wood as a renewable energy source, resulting in growing exports of wood pellets from the United States and Canada to Europe (Searchinger and Heimlich 2015, p. 26). Nor does the EU expect to implement sustainability standards for wood pellets before 2020 (Flach and others 2014, p. 33).

(RFS2) doubled the biofuels mandate to 9 billion gallons in 2008 and set a target of 36 billion gallons by 2022. With food prices already rising when EISA passed, Congress capped the amount of conventional (corn-based) ethanol under the mandate to 15 billion gallons after 2014 and shifted the emphasis to cellulosic biofuels. But cellulosic technology continues to lag and, while the mandate also provides incentives for other advanced biofuels and biodiesel (table 4-3), conventional ethanol still accounts for the vast majority of biofuels consumed in the United States.

In EISA, Congress also added sustainability standards and charged the U.S. Environmental Protection Agency (EPA) with conducting life cycle analyses to determine which "biofuel pathways" (feedstocks and processing methods) would reduce net GHG emissions by enough to be eligible under the mandate. Not only is the assumption of carbon neutrality in life cycle analysis suspect, however, but also the uncertainty surrounding the estimates of indirect land use change effects is large. These issues make the life cycle analysis vulnerable to political influence and open it to controversy. Other obstacles to EISA's stated goals arise from the fact that most automobiles on the U.S. market today cannot easily accommodate ethanol blends higher than 10 percent without risking engine damage. Ethanol producers began running into the "blend wall" as early as 2013,

Table 4-3   RFS2 Mandate Levels/EPA Adjusted Targets in Billions of Gallons

Year	Corn-based ethanol	Biodiesel[a]	Cellulosic biofuels	Total renewable fuels target[b]
2008	9.0	0.0	0	9.00
2009	10.5	0.50	0	11.10
2010	12.0	0.65	0.100/0.0065	12.95
2011	12.6	0.80	0.250/0.0060	13.95
2012	13.2	1.00	0.500/0.00	15.20
2013	13.8	1.00/1.28	1.000/0.006	16.55
2014	14.4/13.5	1.00/1.63	1.750/0.033	18.15/16.28
2015	15.0/13.9	1.00/1.73	3.000/0.123	20.50/16.93
2016	15.0/14.5	1.00/1.90	4.25/0.230	22.25/18.11
2017	15.0/14.8	1.00/2.00	5.50/0.312	24.0/18.8
2022	15.0	1.00	16.000	36.00

Sources: Schnepf and Yacobucci (2013, p. 3); EPA final rules for 2014–16 and the proposed rule for 2017 are available through the RFS website at www.epa.gov/renewable-fuel-standard-program.

a. The mandate for biodiesel sets a minimum of 1 billion gallons per year starting in 2012. Beginning with 2013, the EPA has set a target above the minimum to at least partially make up for reductions in the cellulosic and, more recently, corn-based ethanol targets.

b. The balance between the sum of the values shown and the total is "other advanced biofuels," which can include sugarcane ethanol from Brazil.

which leaves no room to accommodate any cellulosic fuel that makes it to the market and makes it difficult for the EPA to implement the RFS2 as written.

Weaknesses in the Sustainability Standards

As rising commodity prices created incentives to convert forests and other virgin lands to cropland in the late 2000s, policymakers could no longer blithely assume that replacing fossil fuels with the current generation of biofuels would help mitigate climate change. In a partial response, U.S. and EU policymakers adopted sustainability standards for biofuels under their respective mandates. These standards address the potential for unsustainable *direct* land use change by restricting the use of virgin lands for feedstock production, and set standards for minimum emissions reductions, relative to conventional fuels, that biofuels must achieve to count against the mandated targets.

These standards address important issues, but the outcomes of the processes for developing the sustainability criteria appear to reflect the competing interests of domestic feedstock producers. In both the United States and the EU, the principal feedstocks just barely passed the threshold for minimum GHG emissions savings to qualify under each mandate. And that is without taking the potential impact of indirect land use change into account in the European case (box 4-2).

Under the revised U.S. mandate, the EPA is charged with developing a methodology for conducting life cycle analyses and determining which feedstocks and technological pathways would be eligible under the mandate. The net emissions targets specified in U.S. policy include estimates of indirect land use change, but also build off the assumption of carbon neutrality critiqued in recent research.[46] EISA also specifies that eligible feedstocks must come from "renewable biomass," which excludes virgin agricultural land cleared or cultivated after December 2007, as well as tree crops, residues, or other biomass from federal lands. The method of verifying this latter requirement is notably crude, however.[47]

---

46. DeCicco and Krishnan (2015); and Searchinger and Heimlich (2015).

47. While the final rule implementing the RFS has recordkeeping requirements designed to verify compliance with the renewable biomass eligibility requirements (section 80.1454), these requirements are waived for many producers unless the total area of "agricultural land" exceeds the area that was in production in 2007. There is no information readily

Box 4-2   Farm and Industry Influence on EU Sustainability Standards

LIKE THE UNITED STATES, the European Union introduced sustainability standards when it ramped up support for biofuels in the wake of the food price spikes. Those standards prohibit feedstocks produced on land with "high biodiversity value such as primary forests and highly biodiverse grasslands . . . land with high carbon stocks such as wetlands or continuously forested areas . . . [or] peatland."[a] There are also social standards related to the impact on food prices and adherence to International Labor Organization conventions protecting worker rights. Biofuels must also reduce emissions relative to gasoline or diesel by at least 35 percent to be eligible for financial support or count toward the mandate, rising in 2017 to 50 percent for existing plants and 60 percent for new ones.

As in the United States, however, there are hints that protection for domestic constituents played a role in implementing the sustainability standards. The directive tasked the European Commission's Joint Research Centre with estimating the "typical" GHG reductions for various feedstocks using specific production pathways. The European Commission then applied discount factors to these calculations, supposedly so that the default estimates of net emissions reductions would be conservative.[b] Producers using feedstocks where the default calculation does not reach the 35 percent target can submit data to show their process meets the standard. Unlike the U.S. standards, these calculations do not include estimates of the impact of indirect land use change.

Again, as in the United States, where the main ethanol feedstock (corn) just barely passed the threshold for net GHG emissions, rapeseed, the main European biodiesel feedstock, just barely squeaked over the threshold there (table 4-2). Soy-based biodiesel, which likely would be imported or use imported feedstocks, falls just short of the default value at 31 percent. The European estimate of net reductions for soy-based biodiesel is well below that of the U.S. EPA, even though the EPA's estimate includes

---

The EISA requires that net emissions from the production of conventional biofuels be at least 20 percent less than those from gasoline. The emissions reduction threshold for cellulosic biofuels is 60 percent, while

---

available on the EPA website to indicate that the increase in agricultural land, as measured by the RFS requirements, has ever occurred. That is not a guarantee, however, that newly cleared land was not offset by newly fallowed land elsewhere.

indirect land use change. For unknown reasons, researchers also applied a larger discount factor to the typical savings in calculating the default value for soy biodiesel than it did for rapeseed.[c] With rapeseed biodiesel just above the minimum net emissions threshold (38 percent versus the 35 per-cent default level), any consideration of indirect land use change would almost surely disqualify it.[d]

But the EU directive asked only that the Commission review GHG emis-sions associated with indirect land use change by December 2010 and recommend changes to the directive if appropriate. The resulting report concluded that indirect land use change could affect GHG emissions sav-ings from using biofuels, but that there were uncertainties in measuring those effects. The Commission, therefore, determined that it should pre-pare an impact assessment and it commissioned the International Food Policy Research Institute (IFPRI) to conduct it.[e] The IFPRI report concluded that land use changes would eliminate about two-thirds of expected GHG emissions savings from using biofuels.[f] The results summarized in the Commission's impact assessment showed that none of the major biodiesel feedstocks would come close to meeting the directive's 35 percent reduc-tion in net greenhouse gas emissions if the policy incorporated the effects of indirect land use changes.[g] Indeed, rapeseed and soybean oils, along with palm oil not using methane capture during processing, all came out looking *worse* from a climate change perspective than regular diesel.

a. Flach and others (2013, p. 5).
b. Ibid., p. 6.
c. Ibid., p. 8.
d. European Commission (2012, pp. 26–27).
e. Ibid., p. 6.
f. Laborde (2011).
g. European Commission (2012, p. 26).

other advanced biofuels and biodiesel must achieve a net reduction of at least 50 percent. The EPA determined that corn ethanol produced using natural gas, biomass, or biogas and designated technologies would reduce emissions by 21 percent, just past the 20 percent threshold for conven-tional biofuels. Sugar and sorghum, again using certain technologies and cleaner energy sources for processing, meet the standard for advanced biofuels.

Even with these EISA requirements, there is an important loophole. Congress did not want to create stranded assets, so EISA exempts ethanol plants from the net 20 percent reduction in emissions if construction on these plants had started before December 2007. Plants that use natural gas or biomass for processing and where construction was begun between 2007 and 2009 are also exempt from the emissions reduction threshold.[48] According to the EPA, most corn ethanol capacity was grandfathered and thus is exempt from the minimum GHG reduction target, although these plants must still comply with the other requirements, including the statute's prohibition on the conversion of virgin land for feedstock production.[49] Given all the exemptions and caveats, and the misguided assumption of carbon neutrality, it is difficult to conclude with any confidence that corn ethanol is contributing much, if anything, to reducing GHG emissions.

The EPA also approved soybean, canola, and rapeseed oils as eligible feedstocks for biodiesel, which had new targets under the RFS2 mandate. However, the EPA analysis concluded that land use changes would wipe out the GHG emissions savings from using palm oil, and consequently it is not currently an eligible feedstock under RFS2. A petition asking the EPA to reconsider the palm oil decision remains under review, however, and some palm oil is apparently being used in U.S. biodiesel. Appendix A provides rough estimates of biodiesel-related demand for palm oil in the United States and the EU (where demand is far larger). Policies contributing to this demand are a particular concern because of the potential for significant increases in GHG emissions due to deforestation and conversion of peatlands in Southeast Asia.[50]

Finally, the calculations of net emissions from biofuels are complex and rely on a number of questionable assumptions. In the case of the EPA's analysis of life cycle emissions from various feedstocks, the estimates changed substantially between the time that the initial rule was posted for public comment and when the final rule was published. In the initial EPA

48. Schnepf and Yacobucci (2013, p. 8).

49. See question 7 under section 3 of "Questions and Answers on Changes to the Renewable Fuel Standard Program (RFS2)" on the EPA's website at www.epa.gov/otaq/fuels/renewablefuels/compliancehelp/rfs2-aq.htm#4.

50. Persson, Henders, and Kastner (2014); and Elliott (2015b).

analysis, neither soy biodiesel nor corn ethanol would have achieved the net emission reductions that the RFS2 requires, but both fuels did pass the threshold when the final rule was published, primarily because of sharply lower estimates of the impact on indirect land use change. Moreover, Yacobucci and Bracmort point out that, in the final EPA ruling, corn ethanol just barely qualified for inclusion, with net life cycle emissions estimated to be 21 percent lower than gasoline. Appendix table A-1 at the back of the ruling showed corn ethanol with net emissions savings of 19 percent, just below the 20 percent threshold. An EPA official told the authors that the latter figure was a typo.[51] The slim margin by which the main European feedstock, rapeseed, passed the EU standard adds to the impression that politics played a role in these calculations (box 4-2).

Ethanol Hits a Wall

Before the ink was even dry on the 2007 legislation expanding the U.S. biofuel mandate, a number of challenges emerged. While farmers and biofuel investors celebrated the boon to their business, the spikes in commodity prices that were emerging even as Congress passed EISA generated a backlash from a variety of other constituencies. At the peak of the food price spikes in 2008, Texas governor Rick Perry unsuccessfully petitioned the EPA for a partial waiver of the mandate to alleviate the impact on corn and other livestock feed prices.[52] Development advocates protested the negative impact on food security in vulnerable countries, while growing numbers of environmentalists expressed concerns about the effects on GHG emissions and biodiversity if biofuel demand contributed to deforestation or other land use changes in sensitive areas.

In the face of this growing opposition, the only major change to American biofuel support policies so far has been due to budget pressures. When Congress created the RFS, it initially left the $0.45 per gallon tax credit for blending ethanol with gasoline in place. With the mandate's floor under demand supporting ethanol investments, and rising oil prices spurring

---

51. Yacobucci and Bracmort (2010, pp. 15–16).

52. When drought sent corn prices soaring again in 2012, the governors of Arkansas and North Carolina requested another waiver because of the impact of high feed costs on their poultry and pork producers The EPA again declined to take action.

demand, the cost of the tax credit escalated. At the end of 2011, with the annual cost at $6 billion and rising, Congress let the tax credit expire.[53]

Even without the tax credit, and regardless of the mandate, refiners had reasons to continue blending ethanol with gasoline. As noted, ethanol is the cheapest available additive for meeting Clean Air Act regulations on gasoline additives. That regulation puts a floor under ethanol demand of 5 percent to 6 percent of gasoline consumption. The high octane levels of ethanol also allow refiners to use cheaper, lower-octane blendstocks to produce gasoline so market demand will rise when corn prices are low relative to oil prices.[54] Depending on relative prices for ethanol and gasoline, ethanol demand could continue at around 10 percent even without the government mandate. Sharply falling oil prices in 2015 put pressure on ethanol demand and profits, however, and if sustained will give the mandate a more important role in sustaining demand.

Beyond 10 percent blend levels (E10), current technology and infrastructure work against higher demand for ethanol. Until 2011, EPA regulations limited the ethanol content of gasoline to 10 percent when used in unmodified vehicles because of concerns about engine damage. Modified "flex-fuel" vehicles can safely use blends up to 85 percent, but few of those are in operation in the United States and there are few places to buy E85. The corrosive properties of ethanol also mean that higher blends require separate pipelines, fuel tanks, and other delivery infrastructure. In effect, these technological and infrastructure constraints create an ethanol "blend wall" at around 10 percent.

When the mandate was revised upward in 2007, U.S. gasoline consumption was 142 billion gallons and the Energy Information Administration projected 1 percent annual growth for the foreseeable future. With the conventional ethanol cap set at 15 billion gallons, Congress did not anticipate problems with this "blend wall" because it expected ethanol consumption to remain below the 10 percent limit. Instead, rising gasoline prices and increased fuel economy standards for cars (also in EISA) caused

53. Schnepf (2013, pp. 30–31).

54. See Schnepf (2013, pp. 4–5) and Abbott (2013, p. 8); see also "Higher RIN Prices Support Continued Ethanol Blending despite Lower Gasoline Prices," U.S. Energy Information Administration, February 23, 2015, www.eia.gov/todayinenergy/detail.cfm?id=20072.

annual U.S. gasoline consumption to drop to around 135 billion gallons. That meant that refiners began bumping up against the blend wall in 2013–14 (figure 4-3).[55] From the perspective of energy security, it should also be noted that EISA's conservation measures reduced fossil fuel use from its projected level by roughly the same amount as the biofuel mandate has done. And Obama administration regulations require even higher fuel efficiency standards, which (if implemented) will further reduce the demand for transportation fuels and reduce GHG emissions.[56]

To at least partially address the blend wall, the EPA raised the permitted blend level for vehicles built in 2001 or later to 15 percent (E15). Automobile manufacturers, however, mostly declined to recognize E15 as safe for model years earlier than 2013. They warned that warranties might not be valid on older vehicles if E15 caused engine damage. In addition, having different blends for different model-year vehicles would mean that gasoline stations would have to invest in new pumps and storage tanks. Not surprisingly, since consumers are not vocally demanding E15, there is little interest on the part of retailers to spend the money (Energy Information Administration 2012, 5). In addition, E15 is not approved for other engines. Producers of recreational motor boats, lawn mowers, and other products using smaller engines dislike the mandate because of potential corrosion damage to their products, even at current blend levels.[57] Thus, ethanol consumption will only increase substantially more in the United States if the government provides additional subsidies to build the infrastructure and promote flex-fuel vehicles that can use higher ethanol blends, as the industry is demanding.

The EPA has encountered even greater problems trying to implement the mandate for cellulosic biofuels because supplies have been far below what Congress expected (table 4-3). EPA regulators tried to provide a push to the industry by setting targets that were a stretch. But refiners filed and

---

55. CBO (2014, pp. 7–8).

56. Driving and gasoline consumption did turn back up when gasoline prices dropped sharply in 2015–16. A variable gasoline tax set to maintain minimum prices and prevent such swings in behavior would help to preserve conservation gains.

57. The Renewable Fuels Association provides information for boat and classic car owners on steps they should take to protect engines from ethanol damage on its website, www. ethanolrfa.org/.

Figure 4-3   Corn Ethanol Mandate Level and Consumption under RFS2

Billions of Gallons

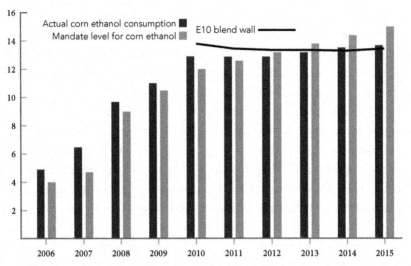

Sources: Schnepf and Yacobucci (2013, p. 3) for mandates and EPA adjustments; Renewable Fuels Association Statistics for actual ethanol consumption are available at "World Fuel Ethanol Production," http://ethanolrfa.org/resources/industry/statistics/; data for the proposed adjustments to the 2014 mandate are available at L. L. Bergeson, "White House Weighs Higher EPA 2014 RFS Targets to Help Climate Efforts," BRAG Biobased Products Blog (July 18, 2014), http://blog.braginfo.org/entry/white-house-weighs-higher-epa-2014-rfs-targets-to-help-climate-efforts/; the blend wall level is based on 2014 EIA projections as reported in the CBO report.

Notes: Actual ethanol consumption for 2015 is extrapolated from data on the first seven months from RFA.

won lawsuits challenging the EPA when they were faced with millions of dollars in fines for not blending biofuels that did not exist in the market.[58] By sometime in 2015, plants capable of producing 75 million gallons or so are expected to be online, up from 6 million gallons in 2011. Yet, even with that growth, the gap with the formal EISA targets—3 billion gallons in 2015 and 16 billion gallons by 2022—continues to grow. And now, the blend wall is raising questions about how the market can absorb larger amounts of advanced biofuels if they become available.[59]

58. Wald (2012).

59. See Krauss (2014) and Schnepf and Yacobucci (2013, 3).

In 2013, the American Petroleum Institute and another industry group filed a petition asking the EPA to partially waive the mandate with respect to conventional ethanol, as well as cellulosic biofuels, because of the growing difficulties presented by the blend wall. At the end of 2013, with the conventional ethanol target rising to 14.4 billion gallons and the Energy Information Administration projecting that U.S. gasoline consumption would fall to just under 133 billion gallons, the EPA took the unprecedented step of proposing reductions in the overall target for renewable fuels, as well as that for cellulosic biofuels (table 4-3). On November 21, 2014, after receiving an avalanche of comments on the proposal, the EPA announced that it would not set the targets for either 2014 or 2015, due at the end of November 2013 and 2014, respectively, until sometime in 2015.[60]

In early 2015, Senators Dianne Feinstein (D-Calif.), Pat Toomey (R-Penn.), and Jeff Flake (R-Ariz.) reintroduced legislation to eliminate the corn ethanol mandate, criticizing it as "unwise and unworkable."[61] Representative Bob Goodlatte (R-Va.) introduced similar legislation in the House with the support of nearly five dozen colleagues, as well as introducing another bill to repeal the RFS entirely.[62] In November 2015, just before the EPA was scheduled to release the final RFS target numbers for 2014–16, two subcommittees of the House Committee on Science, Space, and Technology held a hearing to review 10 years of costs and benefits under the RFS legislation, with the subcommittee chairs expressing skepticism.[63] None of the biofuel reform legislation moved in 2015, and there was never much chance that it would do so in 2016, an election year.

60. "EPA Says It Will Not Act on 2014 RFS until 2015, Industry Offers Mixed Reactions," *Agri-Pulse*, November 21, 2014, www.agri-pulse.com/EPA-says-it-wont-act-on-RFS-until-2015-industry-offers-mixed-reactions-112114.asp (accessed January 10, 2017).

61. See the February 26, 2015, press release on Dianne Feinstein's Senate website at www.feinstein.senate.gov/public/index.cfm/2015/2/toomey-feinstein-introduce-bill-to-repeal-ethanol-mandate (accessed November 3, 2015).

62. Links to the bills are available on the energy issues page of Bob Goodlatte's House website, goodlatte.house.gov/issues/issue/?IssueID=14892 (accessed January 10, 2017).

63. See the November 3, 2015, hearing of the Subcommittee on Oversight and Subcommittee on Environment Hearing on "Renewable Fuel Standard: A Ten-Year Review of Costs and Benefits," at https://science.house.gov/legislation/hearings/subcommittee-oversight-and-subcommittee-environment-hearing-renewable-fuel (accessed November 3, 2015).

In late November 2015, the EPA finally published RFS mandate levels for 2014, 2015, and 2016 that represented a compromise, but with a tilt in favor of the biofuel industry. For 2014 and 2015, the EPA set the targets for most categories of biofuels, including the overall mandate level, at about the levels of actual production and below the statutory levels. The one exception was biodiesel. Diesel is far less commonly used in the United States and biodiesel is more expensive to produce than ethanol. When Congress added specific biodiesel targets under RFS2, it set the target at a minimum of 1 billion gallons per year, starting in 2012.[64] In recent years, the EPA has steadily increased the biodiesel target to cushion the reductions in other parts of the mandate, despite its economic and environmental inefficiency (see appendix A).

In making the 2015 decisions, the EPA also got some "help"—albeit perverse from an environmental perspective—from lower oil prices. The sharp drop in prices in 2015 and 2016 contributed to increased gasoline consumption and eased the blend wall constraint. For 2016 and 2017, the EPA final and proposed rules will keep the level for corn-based ethanol below the statutory level but push it to 14.8 billion gallons. Unless gasoline consumption increases more than it has thus far, it is not clear how the market will absorb that much ethanol.[65]

The EU is not facing the same technical challenges, but there was a stronger backlash against its biofuel policy from environmental and development constituencies concerned about deforestation and food security. A European Commission proposal to cap food-based biofuels at roughly the current consumption level triggered strong pushback from farm groups and the biofuel industry, which was operating at far less than full capacity. Ultimately, policymakers adopted a compromise that lowered the ceiling for food-based biofuels while still allowing modest additional growth to avoid large stranded assets. Box 4-3 summarizes this experience, which could be a model for partial U.S. reform.

---

64. Congress also left in place an earlier $1 per gallon tax credit, without which biodiesel is not profitable. See Schnepf (2013, pp. 21–24) for the history of U.S. programs.
65. Irwin and Good (2016).

Box 4-3   European Opposition to Biofuels Forces Partial Reform

IN EUROPE, THE CONFLUENCE of food price spikes and increased government support for biofuels sparked a stronger backlash than in the United States. In addition to concerns from development advocates and environmental groups, biodiesel is also relatively more costly than ethanol. The need for ever costlier subsidies led several member states, notably France and Spain, to pare back national incentives for biofuels.[a] In the face of these growing challenges, the European Commission proposed capping food-based biofuels at 5 percent, within an overall EU blend target of 10 percent. Farm and industry groups criticized the proposal for changing the rules in midstream, which would strand investments that had been made in the expectation of continued support and higher demand. Environmentalists criticized the proposal because it did not go far enough and require policymakers to consider indirect land use change when evaluating biofuels against the sustainability criteria.

After much back and forth between the European Commission, Parliament, and member states over the next four years, the parties agreed to a compromise to cap food-based biofuels at 7 percent. Member states can choose to set lower national limits. The Commission will also monitor and report on indirect land use change, but this will still not factor in the calculations of net GHG emission reductions.[b]

In addition to that relatively modest reform, the European Commission released a new plan for EU energy and environment policies to 2030 that eschews new targets for renewable energy use in the transport sector. The Commission concluded that it had become "clear that first-generation biofuels have a limited role in decarbonising the transport sector."[c] Also in early 2014, the Commission issued guidelines that prohibit public support for investments in new or existing capacity for the production of food-based biofuels and allow operating support for existing capacity only until existing plants are fully depreciated, or the end of 2020, whichever comes first.[d]

a. Flach and others (2013, pp. 13–16).
b. See Casigne (2015).
c. European Commission (2014a, pp. 6–7).
d. European Commission (2014b, p. 24).

HOLDING THE LINE ON FOOD-BASED BIOFUELS

Given the fracking boom's impact on domestic oil production and the growing questions about GHG emissions from biofuels, policymakers can no longer justify support for first-generation biofuels on the basis of either energy security or climate change mitigation. Moreover, current policy may inhibit further development of cellulosic and other next-generation biofuels that might do more to help mitigate climate change. The United States today is by far the largest market for biofuels, but they are still overwhelmingly food-based, first-generation fuels with little scope to expand in the absence of government mandates and subsidies for infrastructure.

Despite the growing evidence that this generation of food-based biofuels is no better, and oftentimes worse, than fossil fuels for the climate, the policy survives because it is yet another mechanism to support the incomes of some American farmers, and now also those of biofuel producers that would be far fewer and smaller without billions of dollars in subsidies. Not surprisingly, farm and biofuel industry groups are vigorously fighting efforts to roll back mandates and subsidies.

The biofuel industry has an argument that they invested because the government encouraged them to do so, and that they should not have to bear all the adjustments costs because things have changed. But that does not justify additional subsidies for retail and distribution infrastructure to help the industry get over the blend wall and expand further. Moreover, even without the RFS mandate, the ethanol industry will survive. Somewhere between 5 percent and 10 percent of gasoline would have to be ethanol to meet Clean Air Act regulations, with the ratio varying with relative corn and oil prices. That puts a floor under the market and would stem the losses even if Congress eliminates the mandate.

If eliminating the mandate completely proves too politically difficult, Congress could follow a course similar to what the EU did in amending its mandate. The EU reform capped support for first-generation, food-based biofuels at a bit above current consumption levels, which shields the industry from large capital losses, but also limits further growth.[66]

---

66. Elliott (2015b) provides more detail on how changes to the mandate could work to maintain incentives to develop advanced biofuels while limiting the growth of corn ethanol.

Further USDA subsidies for pipelines, new gas station pumps, or other infrastructure that helps corn ethanol producers get around the blend wall and expand further are precisely the wrong direction.

In sum, U.S. (as well as European and other) policies promoting biofuels make it more difficult to save the world's forests, slow climate change, and ensure that the world's poor are adequately fed. Even without considering land use change, many of the current biofuels, including corn-based ethanol, may well be responsible for more GHG emissions than gasoline or diesel. It is past time to admit that biofuel policies, however well intentioned, were a mistake, most notably for poor countries that are most at risk from climate change and volatile food markets.

5

LIVESTOCK SUPPORT AT THE
EXPENSE OF GLOBAL HEALTH

THE UNITED STATES IS THE world's largest exporter of meat and its third largest producer. U.S. producers account for a third of global exports of pork and poultry, and a sixth of beef exports. These producers get less in the way of *direct* subsidies or protection than the livestock sectors of many other rich countries. But the U.S. government provides a range of *indirect* subsidies by failing to tax or regulate negative spillovers associated with livestock production, which lowers costs and encourages consumption. The subsidies for corn and soybeans discussed earlier also lower feed costs for livestock producers.

Some of the negative spillovers from livestock operations are local in scope, such as water pollution from mismanagement of wastes, but others are global. And some of the global public "bads" generated by meat production are particularly costly for developing countries. A major one is climate change, to which livestock contributes directly through methane emissions from animals and indirectly through the conversion of forests for grazing land. The United Nations Food and Agriculture Organization estimates that, across the entire life cycle, the livestock industry directly and indirectly accounts for as much as 14 percent of global greenhouse gas emissions (see appendix B).

The focus of this chapter is on the widespread use of antibiotics in livestock operations and the role that such use is playing in the global spread of antibiotic-resistant bacteria. Before the discovery of antibiotics in the early 20th century, even minor injuries could be deadly if an infection set in.[1] Surgery and cancer treatments would be far riskier without antibiotics to prevent infection. But the more we use them, the faster bacteria adapt and become resistant to the drugs' effects. The Centers for Disease Control and Prevention estimate that two million people become sick and 23,000 die each year in the United States from antimicrobial-resistant infections. Globally, the number could be more than 700,000 people.[2] Drug resistance is now spreading so rapidly that there is talk of a nightmarish post-antibiotic future where minor cuts again turn deadly.

Antibiotic-resistant bacteria are a threat to all of us. But the greatest danger is in poor countries where respiratory infections and diarrheal diseases remain leading causes of death, especially for children.[3] The second- and third-line drugs to which doctors turn when initial treatments fail are also generally more expensive, and are liable to strain the resources of already weak public health systems in developing countries and leave the poor with few options.[4] The 2014 O'Neill review on antimicrobial resistance, commissioned by British prime minister David Cameron, estimated that under current trends ten million more people would die prematurely each year from drug-resistant infections. The global economy would also be $60 trillion to $100 trillion smaller by 2050, and developing countries in Africa and Asia would bear the brunt of these burdens.

While the inappropriate use of antibiotics in human health is a key factor in accelerating the emergence of drug resistance, livestock producers use large amounts of antibiotics in ways that allow resistant bacteria

---

1. Antibiotics are part of the broader antimicrobial drug category, and some studies and data sources use the broader label. Yet the key concerns, especially with respect to agricultural uses, relate to antibiotics, and that is the focus here.

2. Review on Antimicrobial Resistance (2014, pp. 8–9).

3. The World Health Organization presents data on the top ten causes of death in 2012, by income group, atwww.who.int/mediacentre/factsheets/fs310/en/index1.html (accessed February 9, 2015).

4. Nugent, Back, and Beith (2010, pp. 17–19).

to thrive.[5] Farmers also use drugs that often are either the same as or chemically related to drugs used in human health. The European Union a few years ago, and the United States more recently, began to take steps to reduce antibiotic use in livestock, especially where antibiotics are used to promote more rapid growth. But the American response so far has been relatively slow and timid. The livestock industry in the United States is even resisting the collection of more detailed data so that policymakers can better understand the scope of the problem and identify priorities for addressing it.

Before turning to the role of agriculture in antibiotic resistance, it is useful to review recent trends in livestock production and trade—and the role of government subsidies in encouraging them. The chapter then turns to the current state of knowledge about antibiotic use in livestock and the implications for antibiotic resistance and human health. After reviewing what U.S. policymakers are and are not doing to address the problem, it examines evidence suggesting that the costs of forgoing the routine use of antibiotics for nontherapeutic purposes would not be costly for most livestock producers.

LIVESTOCK SUBSIDIES, CONSUMPTION, AND TRADE

The United Nations Food and Agriculture Organization projects that the consumption of animal products will increase more than 70 percent by 2050, with most of the growth occurring in developing countries. Trade in meat and livestock is also growing rapidly, mostly due to rising incomes in developing countries that allow people to add more protein to their diets. This trade also creates new avenues to transmit antibiotic resistance globally.

While the United States is by far the largest meat consumer on a per capita basis, average consumption is declining slightly, as it is in the EU. Americans are also eating more chicken and less beef, which reduces the climate change impact. The consumption growth is in Brazil, China, and other emerging markets. Russian consumption is also recovering from

5. Antibiotics are also used for disease prevention in aquaculture and horticulture, but the total amounts are small relative to livestock; see Hollis and Ahmed (2013, p. 2475).

the sharp drop in incomes after the Soviet Union's collapse.[6] India currently consumes very little meat, but, among developing countries, it is a large and growing consumer of dairy products. The FAO also projects that India's poultry consumption will increase sharply, though the magnitude is uncertain because of poor data quality.[7]

The United States is the world's largest producer of beef and poultry, and the third-largest producer of pork, behind China and the EU (figure 5-1a). The United States and the EU together account for two-thirds of the world's exports of pork and the United States and Brazil for two-thirds of poultry exports (figure 5-1b). Interestingly, India, which consumes very little beef for religious and cultural reasons, recently passed Brazil and Australia to become the world's largest exporter of beef (some from buffalo). The United States is fourth largest. This suggests that cooperation on livestock management from a relatively small number of countries could go far in addressing the antibiotic use problem.

To meet growing demands for animal products over the years, major producers have long been moving to larger, more specialized and intensive production models.[8] By 2005, an estimated three-quarters of the world's poultry supply, two-fifths of its pork, and two-thirds of all eggs came from large, intensive livestock operations. Moreover, "virtually all of the growth in livestock production is occurring in industrial systems," especially in developing countries.[9]

To get the flavor of what this means, consider the changes in U.S. livestock operations over the past five decades. The average number of cattle and chickens on American farms and ranches doubled; the inventory of the average pork producer increased from 49 animals in 1964 to 1,100 in 2012. And these averages vastly understate the degree of concentration. For example, two-thirds of hogs and pigs are produced on just 5 percent of swine operations, with an average of 15,000 animals per farm; large poultry operations typically raise nearly 1 million birds per year.[10] More

---

6. Data are from the Food and Agriculture Organization's online database.

7. Robinson and Pozzi (2011, p. viii); and Alexandratos and Bruinsma (2012, pp. 56–57).

8. NRC (1999); and Center for a Livable Future (2013, p. vii).

9. Naylor and others (2005, p. 1621).

10. USDA, 2012 Census of Agriculture.

Figure 5-1a Top Producers of Beef, Pork, and Poultry, 2014 (Millions of Metric Tons)

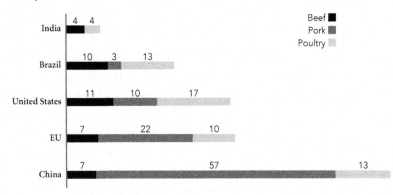

Source: FAO Statistics Division, FAOSTAT Production database.

Note: Pork production in India is negligible.

Figure 5-1b Top Exporters of Beef, Pork, and Poultry, 2014 (Millions of Metric Tons)

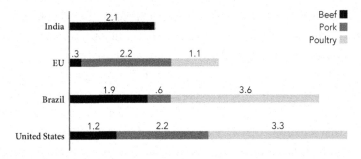

Source: FAO Statistics Division, FAOSTAT Production database.

Note: Pork exports for India are negligible.

intensive production is more efficient, particularly in using less land. But it also contributes to air and water pollution. And, increased livestock densities make disease management a critical concern, often leading to an increased demand for antibiotics.

The intensive production model is also spreading rapidly in emerging economies. China is the world's largest meat producer by far (figure 5-1a) and one recent report estimates that the share of Chinese pork produced by "factory farms" rose from 2.5 percent in 1985 to 22 percent in 2007.[11] A researcher at the Chinese Academy of Sciences (CAS) cited estimates that China consumes a total of 150,000 to 200,000 metric tons (MT) of antibiotics each year (roughly ten times U.S. levels), with about half of the total going to livestock (mostly pigs).[12] At the end of 2014, the China Central Television network reported that large amounts of antibiotics, "up to four times the legal limit in the United States," were found in China's major rivers and in some cities' tap water.[13] A pharmaceutical company admitted to dumping antibiotics in rivers near its production facilities. But CAS researchers, using genetic analysis, identified farms as the major source. In 2011, China's Ministry of Agriculture announced plans to ban the use of antibiotics to promote growth in livestock and to require a veterinary prescription for antibiotic use. China's food system has been scarred by a number of scandals in recent years, however, and it is unclear how effectively this regulation will be implemented.[14]

India, like many developing countries, only loosely regulates antibiotic use in people as well as animals, and it has a growing drug-resistance problem. The *New York Times* reported in late 2014 that 58,000 infants had died in India the previous year because antibiotic treatments had failed. According to the chair of the neonatology department at a prominent New Delhi hospital, the share of babies they were seeing with infections that were multidrug resistant had grown from almost none to nearly all of them over the previous five years. The article quoted one researcher as saying that the problem was due to "India's dreadful sanitation, uncontrolled use of antibiotics and overcrowding coupled with a complete lack

11. Schneider (2011, pp. 6–7).

12. Larson (2015, p. 704). As discussed below, other estimates for China suggest much smaller consumption. But those estimates also show that it is already higher than in the United States and projected to grow by much more. These differences underscore the need for better data.

13. See "Maxine Builder: Antibiotics in China's Rivers—An Emerging Health Threat," Asia Unbound Blog, Council on Foreign Relations, January 16, 2015, http://blogs.cfr. org/asia/2015/01/16/maxine-builder-antibiotics-in-chinas-rivers-an-emerging-health-threat/.

14. Larson (2015). See also the special topic page on "China Food Scandals" on the *South China Morning Post* website: www.scmp.com/topics/china-food-scandals. In addition to concerns about resistance, antibiotic residues in meat and other food products can be a problem in countries with relatively weak regulatory systems.

of monitoring." The article also noted that antibiotic use is common in the rapidly growing poultry industry, and it pointed to a study that found antibiotic residues in 40 percent of chicken samples.[15]

The trends in meat production make addressing the externalities associated with livestock production, including antibiotic resistance, particularly important and urgent. Far from addressing those externalities, however, many countries protect and subsidize their meat and dairy producers. Even the EU, which has undertaken significant agricultural policy reforms, still provides relatively high support to beef and chicken producers. Moreover, the figures in table 5-1 understate the degree of producer support, including in the United States, because they do not include support for livestock as a group or for agriculture as a whole, such as irrigation and energy subsidies. Support for grain and soybean producers in the United States and other countries also provides an indirect subsidy to the livestock industry by lowering the cost of feed.[16] Increasingly, governments in developing countries are also supporting meat and dairy producers.

More important, these data miss the implicit subsidies that arise from the failure to control or tax the negative spillovers associated with live-

Table 5-1   Government Support for Producers by Commodity, Average 2011–13

| Commodity | Producer support as a share of gross farm receipts (percent) | | | | | | |
	EU	Japan	Korea	U.S.	Brazil[a]	China[a]	Russia[a]
Beef and veal	29	38	31	0	1	13	26
Milk	6	61	51	6	15	24	18
Pig meat	1	64	55	0	4	13	52
Poultry meat	18	10	42	0	0	2	19

Source: OECD, Producer and Consumer Support database.

a. Data for Brazil, China, and Russia represent average for 2010–12; data for all other countries are an average for 2011–13.

15. Harris (2014).

16. Of course, this benefit has been undercut in recent years by biofuel policies that raise the cost of livestock feed, as discussed in chapter 4.

stock production. In addition to antibiotic resistance, these spillovers can include local problems, such as air and water pollution, and other global public bads, such as large GHG emissions.[17] Thus, while the United States does not provide large, direct subsidies to the livestock sector, its status as one of the largest producers and exporters of meat makes its failure to move more aggressively to regulate antibiotic use a global problem. The relatively muted U.S. response also stands in contrast to the more aggressive efforts to date in Europe.

ANTIBIOTICS ON THE FARM AND AGRICULTURE'S ROLE IN DRUG RESISTANCE

In the 1940s, agricultural scientists inadvertently discovered that animals given feed containing certain antibiotics grew faster and needed less feed per pound of meat produced (called feed efficiency). Although the mechanism by which this happens is not fully understood, the U.S. Food and Drug Administration (FDA) approved the use of antibiotics without a prescription in feed and water shortly thereafter.[18] Regulators across Europe followed a similar path.[19] As a result, farmers began routinely administering small doses of certain antibiotics for extended periods of time to all or most of their animals, which is a recipe for stimulating the growth of drug-resistant bacteria.[20]

There is ample evidence that antibiotic use in agriculture adds to the pool of drug-resistant bacteria in farm animals. The key questions relate to the magnitude of the risk to human health, and the size of the economic benefits from using antibiotics for growth promotion and disease prevention. If the benefits to livestock producers are relatively small and the risks to human health are high, even if uncertain, then the case for action is stronger. Because of the gaps in monitoring and surveillance, and the complexity of the links, there is still a lot we do not know about the links between antibiotic resistance in farm animals and drug-resistant

17. FAO (2006).
18. Mathew, Cissell, and Laimthong (2007, p. 116).
19. Cogliani, Goossens, and Greko (2011, p. 274).
20. WHO (2012a, p. 51).

infections in humans.[21] But the potential risks for human health are high enough to merit serious attention. Moreover, as we will see below, there is a growing body of research that finds the economic gains to farmers from using antibiotics are less than previously thought.

Antibiotic Use on the Farm

While livestock producers started routinely using antibiotics in their animals because of the growth effects, the move to more intensive production systems gave them another reason to do so. With increased density a key feature of industrial feeding operations, diseases could spread very quickly among animals. Farmers began using antibiotics to prevent disease in healthy animals (prophylaxis), as well as to treat disease.[22] The EU banned antibiotic growth promoters (AGPs) in 2006 and the United States phased out their use in 2017. Both still allow the use of antibiotics for disease prevention, though some EU member countries restrict that as well. Since many of the drugs approved for disease prevention are the same as those used for growth promotion, there is evidence that producers often continue to use antibiotics largely as they had been.

Data on antibiotic use in farm animals are sparse, but the available numbers are strikingly large. The figure most commonly seen in the press is that 80 percent of American antibiotic use by volume is in farm animals. The Centers for Disease Control and Prevention (CDC) concluded in a recent report that more than half the total antibiotics used in the United States each year are used in livestock.[23] According to industry surveys in Europe in the late 1990s, about half of total antibiotic use there was also for animals.[24] In Denmark, even after the government banned AGPs, the total volume of antibiotics used in animals was twice as high as that prescribed for humans.[25]

While it is difficult to compare use in humans and animals because of

21. WHO (2014).

22. Rushton, Ferreira, and Stärk (2014, pp. 10–11) provide more detail on antibiotic uses in various types of animals.

23. CDC (2013, p. 11).

24. Follet (2000, p. 151).

25. National Food Institute, (2012, p. 11).

measurement and dosing differences, the key point is that animal use is large. Overall, the available data show that drug companies sold or distributed around 10,000 metric tons (MT) of antibiotics for use in food animals in 2012 in the United States, and 8,000 MT in Europe.[26] To understand the links between agricultural uses of antibiotics and potential threats to human health, however, we need to know far more than just the aggregate numbers. We also need to know how farmers are using antibiotics—in which animals, when, and for what purposes.

Unfortunately, detailed data on antibiotic use are rare. The Danish Integrated Antimicrobial Resistance Monitoring and Research Program (DANMAP) provides one model. Denmark started monitoring antibiotic use and resistance in animals and humans in the mid-1990s, earlier than most other countries. The DANMAP reports include data on which antibiotics are used in which animal species in what amounts and they integrate this information with data on use and resistance in human health.[27] Surveillance in most of the rest of Europe is improving, but still has far to go. The United States collects only highly aggregated sales data, but nothing on how farmers use antibiotics in livestock. We know even less about antibiotic use in agriculture in most of the rest of the world. Here is the little that we do know.

United States. In 2008, Congress required drug producers to report to the FDA on sales and distribution of antimicrobials for use in food-producing animals. Congress also directed the FDA to issue a summary public report that protects companies' proprietary information.[28] From

26. Neither figure includes ionophores, a class of antibiotics never approved for use in human health and not known to contribute to resistance problems. The total figure for U.S. use as reported by the U.S. Food and Drug Administration is just under 15,000 MT, which includes ionophores (FDA 2014).

27. The National Food Institute (2012) summarizes the Danish approach and illustrates the effects of changes in Danish policy. The DANMAP website, with all of the reports, is available at www.danmap.org (accessed January 14, 2015). Rushton, Ferreira, and Stärk (2014, p. 121) report that Sweden and Norway have similar systems.

28. Under the confidentiality requirements of the law, the FDA can only report independently on "categories with three or more distinct sponsors of approved and actively marketed animal drug products." The effect is that some data are reported in highly aggregated categories. In particular, the FDA cannot report separately on antibiotics approved for growth promotion because of this confidentiality rule.

2009 through 2013, the reports were just a few pages long with one table listing the total volume of drugs for use in animals by antimicrobial class. The 2015 report, by contrast, was fifty-seven pages long and it provides a bit more information on how these drugs are used in American agriculture. There is still no way, however, to know how much of the total was used to promote growth, prevent disease, or to treat sick animals. And, as in Europe, we also do not know how much farmers used in pigs versus chickens or cattle.

According to the 2015 FDA report, the total volume of antimicrobials sold or distributed for use in food animals in 2013 was 33 million pounds, an increase of 17 percent over 2009. The report also reveals that 62 percent of those drugs were in "medically important" drug classes, meaning they are also used in human health. The other 38 percent were mostly in the ionophore class, which are not used in human medicine and which have not been linked to resistance problems. Of the medically important drugs, 98 percent were sold over the counter and 95 percent were administered through either feed or water.

We also know that roughly 70 percent of the medically important drugs had FDA approval to be used for "production purposes"; that is, growth promotion and feed efficiency. Many of those same drugs, however, are approved for therapeutic purposes (treatment or prophylaxis). A 1995 study by the now-defunct Office of Technology Assessment estimated that 90 percent of the antimicrobials used in livestock were used as prophylactics or for growth promotion.[29] This estimate is consistent with the share administered in feed or water.

Europe. The European Medicines Agency (EMA) published the initial report from the European Surveillance of Veterinary Antimicrobial Consumption (ESVAC) project in 2010.[30] The report provides data on antimicrobial use in the livestock sector by country, drug class, and mode of administration. The EMA is also working to add species-specific data. The 2015 ESVAC report covered twenty-four EU member countries, plus

---

29. Office of Technology Assessment (1995, chap. 7); and Mellon, Benbrook, and Benbrook (2001).

30. EMA (2014, pp. 22–23).

Iceland and Norway, up from just nine in the first report. In addition to total volumes, the project also reports antimicrobial use per "population correction unit" to control for differences in animal numbers and sizes, which makes it possible to roughly compare usage across countries.

Figure 5-2 shows the most recent ESVAC results for selected countries. These data cannot shed light on the prevalence of antibiotic use for growth promotion in the EU because the ESVAC reports began after the 2006 ban. A European industry survey in the late 1990s, however, found that only a third of antibiotic use in livestock was for growth promotion.[31] Some European countries have been collecting data for longer, and the Danish and Dutch national data for the late 1990s suggest that the shares there were higher. The countries at the bottom of figure 5-2 are those that put national restrictions on antibiotic use well before the EU did.

Finally, the ESVAC reports include information on delivery methods that can tell us something about how farmers use antibiotics. These data show that, in 2012, more than a third of antibiotics, on average, were included in "premixes" prepared by feed mills, and more than half were in the form of oral powders or solutions that producers typically add to feed or water themselves.[32] In other words, farmers are still mostly administering these drugs in forms that are appropriate for preventing disease in whole herds or flocks of mostly healthy animals, rather than to treat sick animals. This approach to drug administration also could be a sign that farmers are still using antibiotics for growth promotion, albeit with a different label.

Emerging Markets and Global Consumption Trends. In a 2015 paper, Van Boeckel, Laxminarayan, and others provide rough estimates of global antimicrobial consumption in agriculture. Using projections of the rapidly growing consumption of animal products, mainly in developing countries, they also estimate how much antimicrobial consumption might grow by 2030 if policies do not change. The authors use statistical models to combine data on "livestock densities, economic projections of demand for meat products, and current estimates of antimicrobial con-

31. Follet (2000, p. 151).
32. EMA (2014, p. 25).

Figure 5-2   Sales of Active Ingredients of Antimicrobials
in Selected EU Countries, 2005–14

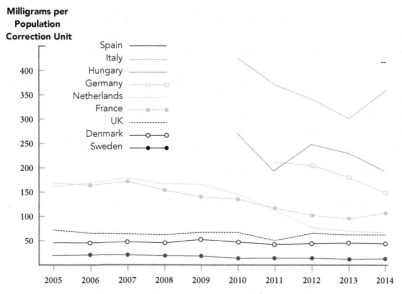

Source: European Medicines Agency, data for 2005 to 2014 compiled from first through sixth ESVAC reports.

Note: The most recent European Surveillance of Veterinary Antimicrobial Consumption (ESVAC) report, released in October 2016, indicates that data reported for Spain for 2011–13 were underestimated; 2014 data included in the most recent ESVAC report were gathered using a new collection system and are estimated at 419 mg/PCU*.

*PCU = Population Correction Unit.

sumption in high-income countries to map antimicrobial use in food animals for 2010 and 2030."[33] They estimate that global antimicrobial use in livestock in 2010 was between 60,000 and 65,000 MT and that it could rise by two-thirds by 2030 if nothing is done. They project that antimicrobial use in Brazil, China, India, Russia, and South Africa will roughly double.

In 2010, the authors estimate that the top five consumers of antimicrobials for livestock production were China, the United States, Brazil, India, and Germany, in that order. By 2030, the authors project that the rankings will be similar, except that Mexico will replace Germany as the fifth-largest overall consumer and China's share of the global total will

33. Van Boeckel and others (2015, p. 1).

rise from 23 percent to 30 percent. Other developing countries will see even faster growth in antimicrobial consumption for livestock, including Indonesia, Nigeria, and Vietnam.[34] Note, however, that other estimates for China suggest that the authors' estimates for that country, and therefore globally, may be significantly understated.[35]

Antibiotic Resistance on the Farm: Risks to Human Health

To sum up, while there is much we do not know, we do know that many farmers and ranchers routinely use large amounts of antibiotics in farm animals and do so in ways that create ideal conditions for the emergence of drug resistance. Many of those drugs are either the same as those used in human medicine or are chemically related.[36] This creates a reservoir of antibiotic-resistant bacteria that can move from animals to humans through a variety of channels:[37]

- To farmers, their families, or employees through direct contact with animals

- To those groups, their neighbors, or others through soil and water contamination (for example, if farmers use manure for fertilizer) or via airborne particles

- To consumers via contaminated meat

Bacteria also pass resistance genes back and forth, creating a mechanism by which antibiotic resistance could be transferred from animal to human pathogens.[38]

In an early study of the potential links, researchers from Tufts University gave poultry a feed mix that was supplemented with tetracyclines. Within just a week, almost all the intestinal flora in the chickens were

34. Ibid., p. 2.

35. See Larson (2015) and Zhu and others (2013).

36. FAO/WHO/OIE (2007).

37. The CDC has a graphic and website discussing the links here: www.cdc.gov/foodsafety/from-farm-to-table.html (accessed March 23, 2015).

38. Rushton Ferreira, and Stärk (2014, pp. 16–21); see Ward and others (2014) for a specific example of gene transfer.

resistant to that antibiotic. Within a few months, a third of fecal samples from human residents on the farm showed they also had higher levels of tetracycline-resistant bacteria than their neighbors (80 percent versus 7 percent).[39] Marshall and Levy summarize the evidence from well over one hundred research studies from around the world that show increased prevalence of drug-resistant bacteria in animals routinely fed antibiotics, and in workers and family members on those farms.[40]

Surveillance systems in the United States and the EU also reveal relatively high rates of drug-resistant bacteria in meat samples, particularly poultry. As part of the National Antimicrobial Resistance Monitoring System (NARMS), the FDA has been monitoring bacteria in retail meats since 2002.[41] The most recent data (for 2011) showed, for example, that 50 percent of retail chicken samples had campylobacter bacteria that were resistant to tetracyclines and 20 percent that were resistant to ciprofloxacin. About half of the salmonella isolates from poultry meat were multidrug resistant.[42] As in the United States, EU surveillance shows that the highest levels of antibiotic-resistant bacteria were usually in poultry meat; for example, around 70 percent of salmonella isolates from chicken and turkey samples showed resistance to ciprofloxacin.[43]

In a particularly intriguing case from Canada, researchers found a strong correlation between changes in antibiotic use in chicken hatcheries and changes in drug-resistant salmonella in retail chicken samples

39. Levy and others (1976).

40. Marshall and Levy (2011).

41. NARMS also tracks changes in the susceptibility to antibiotics of certain intestinal bacteria found in ill people (CDC) and food animals (USDA). The data are available at www.cdc.gov/narms/; see also the FDA's website at www.fda.gov/AnimalVeterinary/Safety Health/AntimicrobialResistance/NationalAntimicrobialResistanceMonitoringSystem /default.htm; and the Agricultural Research Service website at www.ars.usda.gov/Main /docs.htm?docid=6750 (accessed January 14, 2015).

42. The 2014 FDA news release is available at www.fda.gov/AnimalVeterinary/News Events/CVMUpdates/ucm409035.htm; and an interactive data display is available at www.fda.gov/AnimalVeterinary/SafetyHealth/AntimicrobialResistance/NationalAnti microbialResistanceMonitoringSystem/ucm416741.htm (both accessed February 9, 2015).

43. The 2015 report is available at the European Food Safety Authority website at www. efsa.europa.eu/en/efsajournal/pub/4036.htm (accessed March 23, 2015); the European Centre for Disease Prevention and Control also collects data on human antibiotic consumption (ESAC-Net) and resistance (EARS-Net), http://www.ecdc.europa.eu/en/activi ties/surveillance/Pages/index.aspx (accessed January 14, 2015).

and humans.[44] In 2005–07, because of public concerns about rising resistance, Quebec chicken hatcheries voluntarily stopped injecting eggs with a cephalosporin antibiotic that is chemically related to a critically important human drug. The prevalence of resistant salmonella bacteria in retail chicken dropped from over 60 percent to 10 percent in the first year after the ban; in humans, prevalence dropped from 40 percent to almost zero over two years. The incidence of drug-resistant infections in humans also dropped sharply, albeit from very low levels.

The environment is also a potentially important route for transferring drug resistance from animals to humans, as illustrated by the antibiotic-laden rivers in China. But Laxminarayan and others argue that the environmental pathway is understudied.[45] One recent effort to fill this gap is by McEachran and others. The authors found that particulate matter collected downwind of cattle feedlots in the Southern High Plains of Texas carried traces of antibiotics, as well as genes encoded for antibiotic resistance at 400,000 times the levels they had found in upwind samples.[46]

The 2011 Marshall and Levy literature review finds scattered, but compelling, evidence for the transfer of resistance from animals to humans. The key unknown is how often resistant bacteria lead to serious infections in humans.[47] A National Research Council report concluded that:

> A link can be demonstrated between the use of antibiotics in food animals, the development of resistant microorganisms in those animals, and the zoonotic spread of pathogens to humans. The incidence of the spread of human disease in that way is historically very low, but data are seriously inadequate to ascertain whether the incidence is changing.[48]

More than a decade after that report, the systematic data on antibiotic use and resistance in animals and humans that we need to thor-

---

44. Dutil and others (2010).

45. Laxminarayan and others (2013, p. 1069).

46. McEachran and others (2015). On the pushback that some of the Texas Tech University researchers received from the Texas Cattle Feeders Association, see Hershaw (2016).

47. Office of Technology Assessment (1995, chap. 7); and Mathew, Cissell, and Laimthong (2007, p. 126).

48. NRC (1999, p. 8).

oughly assess the risks are still lacking.[49] As Landers and others conclude from their extensive review of the literature, antibiotic use in livestock is "widespread, yet poorly characterized." For example, distinctions between therapeutic, subtherapeutic, and prophylactic uses are not clear and definitions across countries and monitoring systems differ. Overall, the authors find that neither the human risks nor the animal production benefits of antibiotic use are well studied.[50] Even with better data, the link between antibiotic use in food animals and resistant infections in humans is difficult to make definitively because the biological and ecological processes involved are extremely complex.[51]

The dilemma for policymakers is that antibiotic resistance is spreading rapidly *now* and the costs of losing antibiotics as a treatment option would be enormous. And it will take years to collect the necessary data and do further research. Over the past two decades, many countries have created mechanisms to monitor antibiotic use and resistance, and more are doing so. But many countries and the World Health Organization have also concluded that the risks of waiting are too great and they are taking precautionary steps to reduce antibiotic use in agriculture. U.S. policymakers are doing so as well, but the pace of change does not seem to match the urgency of the threat.

(SLOWLY) EVOLVING U.S. POLICIES ON ANTIBIOTIC USE IN AGRICULTURE

One of the first official reports to examine the potential human health hazards of antibiotic use in animals was the Swann Committee in the United Kingdom in the late 1960s. Because of the paucity of hard data, the committee recommended the creation of surveillance programs to track antibiotic use and resistance, as well as precautionary restrictions on antibiotic use in livestock. EU regulators began restricting some antibiotics in the 1970s and banned the use of AGPs entirely in 2006 (box 5-1). American regulators have been constrained by the politics of agricultural policy and only recently moved to restrict the use of antibiotic growth

49. WHO (2012a, p. 50); and Laxminarayan and others (2013, pp. 1061, 1069–70).
50. Landers and others (2012, p. 5).
51. Laxminarayan and others (2013, pp. 1069–71).

promoters, using voluntary guidance to do so. President Obama launched a national strategy to combat antimicrobial resistance in September 2014, but the provisions on agricultural uses are relatively restrained and the surveillance plans weak.

Congress Blocks FDA Action

In the mid-1970s, the FDA undertook a review of safety issues related to using medically important antibiotics to promote growth in farm animals. This would have been the first step toward regulating them, but congressional appropriators directed the FDA to suspend its regulatory actions. Congress called for more research, and the FDA commissioned the National Academy of Sciences to study the issue. That study concluded that the potential hazard to human health from AGPs was "neither proven nor disproven," and that a single study to settle the issue was "technologically impractical." Congressional appropriators directed the FDA to keep its regulatory efforts on hold while further studies were being done.[52]

Nearly 40 years later, amidst lawsuits and petitions from health advocates trying to force its hand, and threats of lawsuits from industry interests if it does take stronger action, the FDA is still struggling with how to regulate antibiotic use in farm animals.[53] Over the past decade, the FDA has begun moving, albeit using "voluntary guidance" for farmers and drug companies. The agency believes the voluntary approach will have quicker impact because any formal regulatory process would get bogged down in lawsuits. In 2014–15, the Obama administration raised the priority of the issue and launched a national strategy to combat antibiotic resistance. The strategy includes provisions related to livestock use, but they do not go much beyond what the FDA is already trying to do.

In 2003, the FDA took a first step and announced that it was unlikely to approve the use of medically important antibiotics in animals in the future. The guidance had no effect on past drug approvals, however, and no apparent effect on use. Figure 5-3 patches together data from the Animal Health Institute (a veterinary drug industry association) and recent FDA reports. It shows continued increases in the total volume of

---

52. National Research Council (1980) and Office of Technology Assessment (1979).
53. Articles by Beinecke (2012) and Krans (2014) indicate the pressures that the FDA is under.

Figure 5-3   Sales of Active Ingredients of Antimicrobials for Food-Producing Animals and Production of Poultry and Red Meat in the United States

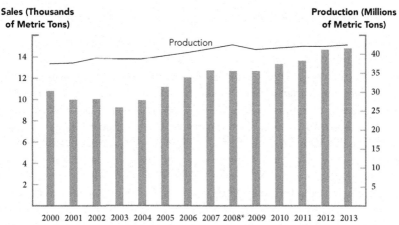

Source: Antimicrobial sales: 2000–2007 from Animal Health Institute Surveys, 2009–2013 from Food and Drug Administration, Department of Health and Human Services, 2015 Summary Report. Production: USDA World Agriculture Supply and Demand Estimates Report.

*Calculated based on simple average between 2007 and 2009.

antibiotics being sold or distributed for use in animals after 2003, even after meat production flattened out.

In 2004–05, the agency prohibited the use in poultry of enrofloxacin because of concerns about the increasing prevalence of drug-resistant campylobacter infections in humans. Enrofloxacin is a fluoroquinolone, a class of second-line drugs, including ciprofloxacin, that the WHO has identified as critically important for human health.[54] Second-line drugs are where doctors must turn when first-line, usually older and cheaper, drugs fail. In 2012, the FDA banned off-label (unapproved) uses of third- and fourth-generation cephalosporins after studies showed routine injections of chicken eggs at hatcheries were promoting salmonella resistance.[55] These drugs are also on the WHO list of critically important drugs.

In 2011 and 2013, the FDA issued two voluntary guidance documents

54. WHO (2012b, p. 26).

55. See the discussion of the Canada case above, and FDA background information on "Extralabel Use and Antibiotics" on the FDA website at www.fda.gov/AnimalVeterinary/SafetyHealth/AntimicrobialResistance/ucm421527.htm (accessed February 11, 2015); see also Center for a Livable Future (2013, p. 9).

Box 5-1   Europe Follows a Precautionary Path

WITHIN A FEW YEARS of the Swann report, European regulators withdrew approval to use key antibiotics—penicillins, tetracyclines, and streptomycin—to promote growth in animals.[a] Farmers could still use these drugs to treat infections in animals and regulators allowed antibiotics approved only for animals to continue being used as feed additives to promote growth. But the latter drugs were often chemically related to antibiotics used for human health. When evidence of resistance to those antibiotics in animals, and of related drugs in humans, began to emerge, European countries gradually tightened the restrictions in the 1990s and 2000s.

Sweden was the first to ban AGPs, acting in 1986 at the behest of Swedish farmers who were concerned about how consumers would react to a report on the heavy use of antibiotics in agriculture.[b] Antibiotic use in farm animals dropped sharply. A decade later, Danish researchers began to document the heavy use of antibiotics in animals and to investigate the links to resistance in animals and humans. Denmark began by ensuring that veterinarians could not profit from the sale of antibiotics to farmers (1995). That immediately cut therapeutic uses of antibiotics by almost half, and overall use by a third.[c] That same year, the government created a system for monitoring antibiotic use and resistance in humans and animals.[d] Danish officials followed with bans on particular AGPs as resistance concerns emerged. Danish pork producers then voluntarily phased out the use of all AGPs in 1998–99, and the government followed with a formal ban in 2000.[e]

Other EU member countries, and ultimately the European Union, followed. EU regulators prohibited the use of all "medically important" antibiotics for growth promotion in 1999 and expanded the ban on using any antibiotic for growth promotion purposes in 2006. Figure 5-2 shows the impact of these restrictions on antibiotic use in countries for which data are available. Sweden and Denmark, which took action well before 2005, are at the bottom and use is relatively stable. The British government undertook education campaigns and encouraged farmers to phase out AGPs well before the EU ban went into effect and use in that country was also relatively low by the mid-2000s.[f] Antibiotic use in Germany, Italy, and Spain, which only recently began reporting on it, remains at far higher

---

levels. Antibiotic use in France declined steadily after the ban while in the Netherlands it initially went up slightly.

The trends in several countries show that antibiotic use for disease prevention or treatment increased after authorities imposed restrictions on AGPs, which forced regulators to take additional steps to rein in use.[g] Figures 5-4 and 5-5 (pp. 122–23) illustrate these trends for Denmark and the Netherlands, where at least some data on AGP use are available before and after the imposition of restrictions. In Sweden, where reductions in overall use stalled after the AGP ban, the government worked with producers to change management practices to improve animal health and, after the mid-1990s, antibiotic use once again began to fall.[h] In Denmark, therapeutic use increased steadily through the 2000s, despite declining swine mortality in the late 2000s.[i] In 2010, Danish authorities introduced the "yellow card" system to identify food producers using quantities of drugs above certain thresholds and get them to take action to reduce consumption.[j] In the Netherlands, after the AGP ban initially produced no change in antibiotic use, the government prohibited the use of antibiotics to prevent disease and set a goal of reducing overall use by 50 percent. They also worked with producers to change husbandry practices and the goal of a 50 percent reduction in antibiotic use was achieved a year early.

a. Cogliani, Goossens, and Greko (2011, p. 278).

b. Ibid., p. 275.

c. Aarestrup (2012, pp. 465–66).

d. Aaerstrup found that veterinarians were earning as much as a third of their income from selling antibiotics to farmers (see Levy 2014, p. A162).

e. Aaerstrup (2012); and Levy (2014).

f. Cogliani, Goossens, and Greko (2011, p. 277).

g. The article by Cogliani, Goossens, and Greko (2011) summarizes lessons from the EU experience; see also Aaerstrup (2012) on Denmark and McKenna (2014) on the Netherlands.

h. Wierup (2001).

i. Aerstrup and others (2010).

j. The Danish Ministry of Food, Agriculture and Fisheries explains this practice on its website at www.foedevarestyrelsen.dk/english/SiteCollectionDocuments/25_PDF_word_filer%20til%20download/Yellow%20Card%20Initiative.pdf (accessed March 26, 2015).

to discourage the use of antibiotics for growth promotion in food animals. In the first document (#209), the FDA, for the first time, formally declared that "the use of medically important antimicrobial drugs for production purposes in food-producing animals does not represent a judicious use of these drugs." The intent was to signal to farmers that they should change their behavior. The second guidance document (#213) followed up by asking pharmaceutical companies to change the labels on medically important antibiotics to remove growth promotion as an approved use.[56] The second guidance document also asked pharmaceutical producers to change drug labels to require veterinary oversight for the remaining approved uses of antibiotics.

As of early 2014, drug companies accounting for virtually all veterinary antibiotic sales had announced their intention to cooperate and to change their labels restricting production and other over the counter uses by end-2016 as requested.[57] As of June 2016, however, the FDA reported that firms had changed or withdrawn only 46 of the 293 previously approved applications affected by Guidance #213. The FDA reported that it had sent a letter to drug manufacturers in May reminding them of the deadline.

But even if the deadline for ending growth promotion applications is met, there is a large loophole arising from the fact that the document allows veterinarians to continue to prescribe antibiotics for group-level use to prevent disease. An analysis by the Pew Charitable Trusts shows that there is significant overlap in the recommended types and dosages of drugs approved for disease prevention and growth promotion:

> About one-quarter of medically important antibiotics (66 of 287) can be used in at least one species for disease prevention at levels fully within the range of growth promotion dosages and with no limit on the duration of treatment. FDA classifies 29 of these 66

56. FDA guidance #213, which also discusses #209, is available for download on the FDA website at www.fda.gov/downloads/AnimalVeterinary/GuidanceComplianceEnforcement/GuidanceforIndustry/UCM299624.pdf. Levy (2014) also discusses the history of the FDA's efforts to reduce AGP use and why it opted for a voluntary approach.

57. The FDA press release is available on the FDA website at www.fda.gov/AnimalVeterinary/SafetyHealth/AntimicrobialResistance/JudiciousUseofAntimicrobials/ucm390738.htm (accessed January 14, 2015).

antibiotics as critically important in human medicine, and 37 as highly important.[58]

Moreover, the experiences in Denmark and the Netherlands show that, without further action, the overall level of antibiotic use may not drop when authorities ban AGPs. The Danish case also suggests that giving veterinarians increased oversight responsibilities may not be effective if they profit from the sale of drugs. In the United States, many veterinarians have financial ties to drug companies and, unlike doctors in human health, there is no requirement to disclose these relationships.[59]

National Strategy to Combat Antibiotic Resistance

In September 2014, the White House released a national strategy to combat antibiotic resistance, based on a report from the President's Council of Advisors on Science and Technology.[60] The PCAST report recommended action to improve surveillance, conserve the efficacy of existing antibiotics through more prudent use in both human health and agriculture, and provide incentives to encourage the development of new antibiotics and alternative treatments.[61]

With respect to antibiotic use in livestock, the report notes that this is "a matter of very serious concern." But the report, and the president's strategy, merely encourage the FDA to vigorously implement the new voluntary guidance documents, to continue to monitor progress by tracking total sales for livestock, and "where possible" to collect data on actual use. Some in Congress introduced legislation authorizing the FDA to go further and collect farm-level data on antibiotic use.[62] But none of those bills has passed.

In March 2015, in anticipation of the World Health Assembly's adoption of a global action plan on antimicrobial resistance, the Obama

---

58. Pew Charitable Trusts (2014, p. 2).

59. Wilson and Dwyer (2014).

60. President Obama's 2014 executive order is available on the White House website at www.whitehouse.gov/the-press-office/2014/09/18/executive-order-combating-antibiotic resistant-bacteria.

61. PCAST (2014, p. 2).

62. See, for example, Grow and Huffstutter (2014).

administration released its National Action Plan for Combating Antibi-otic-Resistant Bacteria (box 5-2). Drawing on the earlier announced na-tional strategy, the action plan is ambitious and detailed in the steps the administration will take to increase stewardship of antibiotics in human health, but it remains exceedingly cautious in tackling antibiotic use in livestock. The plan includes "enhanced monitoring of antibiotic-resistance patterns, as well as antibiotic sales, usage, and management practices, at multiple points in the production chain for food animals and retail meat." But the associated actions were generally at least three years in the future and vague as to what additional data on farm-level antibiotic use will be collected, or how. The FDA held a public meeting in September 2015 and invited public comments through November 30, 2015, to begin the dis-cussion of how to collect more detailed data, but they were still reviewing those comments as of mid-2016 and have no plans to publish the more extensive information before 2018 at the earliest.[63]

The national action plan also calls for the development of educational materials and programs for farmers and veterinarians on "judicious use of antibiotics and antibiotic stewardship." The president's 2016 budget requested a near doubling of funds for combating antibiotic resistance overall and almost four times as much for USDA programs, including for educational programs and for research into alternatives to antibiotics for growth promotion and disease prevention in farm animals.[64] Congress appropriated slightly less overall, $1 billion, but sharply cut the request for USDA funding from $77 million to $26 million.[65] Neither Congress nor the Obama administration has proposed anything to ensure that the incentives facing veterinarians, who will now have a more important role, are aligned with the strategy's public health goals.

63. The FDA's most recent biannual progress report is available on the FDA website at http://www.fda.gov/AnimalVeterinary/NewsEvents/CVMUpdates/ucm509403.htm (accessed August 30, 2016); see also Zuraw (2015).

64. See the White House fact sheet on the White House press office website at www.white house.gov/the-press-office/2015/01/27/fact-sheet-president-s-2016-budget-proposes-historic-investment-combat-a. McKenna (2015) also discusses the budget proposal.

65. See slide 5 of the Presidential Advisory Council presentation on the Department of Health and Human Services website at www.hhs.gov/sites/default/files/us-govern ment-budgets-dedicated-to-combating-antibiotic-resistant-bacteria-activities-here.pdf (accessed August 30, 2016).

EVIDENCE ON THE ECONOMIC EFFECTS OF
RESTRICTING ANTIBIOTIC USE IN AGRICULTURE

American farmers resist further regulation of antibiotics because they fear it would significantly increase their costs. A growing number of studies, however, suggest that improvements in livestock management reduce the need for antibiotics, and that any remaining economic benefits are small when farmers follow good practices. Current antibiotic use practices are rooted in studies that were done before 1990, which found relatively large effects from using antibiotics to promote growth.

Laxminayaran and others reviewed the available research, and they found that the estimated economic benefits from using antibiotics were generally lower in studies conducted since 2000 than they had been in studies before the 1990s. Although the number of more recent studies is relatively small, these authors conclude that the benefits in cattle, pigs, and poultry are substantially lower in modern livestock production systems that use improved nutritional and hygienic practices, and improved breeds.[66] Kansas State University professor Steve Dritz and colleagues have done much of the research on swine production in the United States and Dritz summarizes the key conclusion to be "that the [growth] responses are much lower in magnitude than earlier claims."[67] Research into the impact of AGPs in poultry production has come to similar conclusions.

Evidence from European Restrictions
Though the data still have significant gaps, more direct evidence on the impact of restricting antibiotic use is becoming available as more countries implement AGP bans. In 2011, Cogliani, Goossens, and Greko surveyed the available research on the impact of European restrictions and concluded that "in general, animal food production in these countries continues to thrive, *with appropriate adjustments in practices to ensure continued animal health and safety.*"[68] More detailed research in Sweden, Denmark, and the United States suggests the following effects from restricting AGP use in farm animals:

---

66. Laxminayaran and others (2015, pp. 4–5).
67. Larson (2015, p. 704).
68. Cogliani, Goossens, and Greko (2011, p. 274), emphasis added.

Box 5-2   WHO's Global Action Plan

AFTER ALMOST TWO DECADES of studies, consultations, and strategy development, the World Health Assembly approved a global action plan on antimicrobial resistance in May 2015. The WHO had first published a set of Global Principles for the Containment of Antimicrobial Resistance in Animals Intended for Food in 2000. This was followed in 2001 by a Global Strategy for Containment of Antimicrobial Resistance. Also in 2001, the Codex Alimentarius Commission, which sets global standards for food safety, asked the UN Food and Agriculture Organization and the World Organization for Animal Health (OIE, from the French), along with WHO, to hold a joint expert consultation on these issues.[a]

The 2001 WHO strategy included "rational use in animals" as one of the five most important areas for action, along with surveillance, rational use in humans, infection prevention and control, and innovation in drugs, diagnostics, and other tools.[b] The strategy's recommendations to reduce the risk from the use of antimicrobials in food animals included:

- Require prescriptions for all antimicrobials used for disease control in food animals
- Terminate or rapidly phase out the use of antimicrobials for growth promotion if they are also used in humans
- Create national systems to monitor antimicrobial usage in food animals
- Develop guidelines for veterinarians to reduce overuse and misuse of antimicrobials in food animals

In support of better surveillance and control, the joint FAO/OIE/WHO consultations produced an agreement to identify drugs that should be a priority. As a result, the WHO and the OIE now publish lists of critically im-

---

- little or no impact on productivity or costs in poultry production

- some increased disease in piglets, but little or no impact on productivity in older pigs

- costs associated with adjustments in management practices appear to be small, with some important exceptions.

Wierup examined the Swedish experience, which goes back to the 1980s, and found "no negative clinical effects" of the AGP ban in beef, turkeys, or

portant antimicrobial drugs for human and animal health, respectively.[c] In addition, a 2007 joint experts report identified three classes of critically important drugs for human health (quinolones, third- and fourth-generation cephalosporins, and macrolides), and three foodborne pathogens (Salmonella spp. and Campylobacter spp., and the commensal bacterium *Escherichia coli*) that should be priorities for research and risk assessment.[d]

The WHO 2015 Global Action Plan calls on members to adopt national action plans to address resistance within two years. In a complementary action on livestock use, the OIE created an ad hoc group to make recommendations for a global database on antimicrobial use in animals.[e] The international component of President Obama's national strategy for combating antibiotic resistance calls for coordination with the WHO, the OIE, and the FAO to improve surveillance of antibiotic resistance in animals and food-borne pathogens around the world. It also calls for collaboration to "harmonize international data submission requirements and risk assessment guidelines related to the licensure and/or approval of veterinary medicinal products including antibiotics, vaccines, and diagnostics, to the extent possible."[f]

a. See the description and documents on the UN FAO website at www.fao.org/food-safety-quality/a-z-index/antimicrobial/en/ (accessed January 21, 2015).
b. WHO (2012a, p. 2).
c. The lists can be found online: see WHO (2012b) and OIE (2007).
d. FAO/OIE/WHO (2007, p. viii).
e. There is an OIE conference presentation on the EMA website at www.ema.europa.eu/docs/en_GB/document_library/Presentation/2014/03/WC500162570.pdf (accessed March 25, 2015).
f. Executive Office of the President. (2014, pp. 31–32).

pigs at slaughter, even though antibiotic use dropped by a third. Farmers also used some of the antibiotics approved as growth promoters to prevent a particular disease in chickens (necrotic enteritis), however. Antibiotic use in that sector did not fall until producers made changes in diets and the living environment to prevent the disease, at which total use fell by another third.[69] Wierup found some increased mortality among piglets and that, on average, it took an additional day and a half for a young pig to reach 25 kilo-

69. Wierup (2001).

grams. Feed efficiency was higher, however, among "progressive" producers that used modern management practices and no antibiotics except to treat disease. According to Wierup, researchers had found similar results following AGP bans in Denmark, Finland, and Norway.[70]

Denmark is another country that moved early to restrict antibiotic use in livestock and there have been a number of studies of that experience. The WHO convened an expert group in 2002 to examine the impacts of the Danish measures, and the resulting report broadly confirmed Wierup's findings for Sweden. In poultry, Danish farmers used ionophores to control disease, a class of antimicrobials not used in human medicine, and there was no increase in mortality when the government banned AGPs. Average growth among chickens was also the same after the ban, though feed efficiency dropped a bit over 2 percent.[71] The expert group concluded, however, that the cost of additional feed was offset by the lower cost of not adding antibiotics to it.[72]

The WHO report and Aaerstrup and others also confirm Wierup's findings that there was little impact of removing AGPs on older pigs (finishers), but some negative impact on younger pigs. Aaerstrup and others found little or no impact on total pig production, average weight gain, or feed efficiency in older pigs. One puzzle is that therapeutic use of antibiotics continued to increase modestly even after mortality in swine dropped in the mid- to late 2000s. Aarestrup suggests this could be because the price of antibiotics was dropping.[73]

The experts contributing to the WHO report on Denmark also conducted an economic analysis using available data on relative weight gain, feed efficiency, mortality, and feed and other variable costs. They found that the extra costs associated with the AGP ban were relatively modest, perhaps one additional euro per pig or around 1 percent. Using a general equilibrium model of the Danish economy, researchers found that the AGP ban might have caused a decrease in pig production of 1.4 percent, but a small increase in poultry production of 0.4 percent because of

70. Wierup (2001, pp. 187 and 189).

71. Emborg and others (2001), cited in Aaerstrup (2012, p. 466), find no decline in either the total of chickens produced or the amount of feed used.

72. WHO (2003, pp. 6–8, and 41).

73. WHO (2003); and Aaerstrup and others (2010).

substitution effects. The impact on the Danish economy as a whole was minimal. The report notes that the expert group did not have data on potentially larger, one-time costs related to changes in production systems, such as the costs of modifying animal housing or constructing new buildings. But a communication from the Danish Bacon and Meat Council stated that broader changes in production systems and associated higher capital costs were due to factors other than the AGP ban.[74]

Another indication of the limited competitive impact of the AGP bans in Europe comes from export performance. When the AGP restrictions were imposed there, Denmark was the world's leading pork exporter. It remained so until 2008, a decade after its unilateral AGP ban, when German and American exports began to edge past those of Denmark (figure 5-4). The Netherlands is also a major meat exporter and, after a dip during the global recession in 2009, Dutch exports recovered strongly, despite sharp falls in antibiotic use (figure 5-5).

Recent Research from U.S. Experiments

American researchers examining practices among poultry and swine producers have come to conclusions about the limited benefits of AGPs that are similar to those found in Europe. Engster and others conducted controlled trials for the Perdue poultry company in Maryland and North Carolina. The experiment involved removing AGPs from some flocks but not others that were otherwise treated similarly: housed under the same conditions and fed the same diet. Both sets of flocks continued to receive ionophores to prevent disease. There were no more disease outbreaks in the treatment flock compared to the control group, mortality was just 0.2 percent higher, and there were only small drops in weight gain and feed efficiency in the treatment group (those not receiving AGPs). When other researchers reexamined the data from the experiment and compared the cost of the small losses in growth and feed efficiency to the higher cost of antibiotic-supplemented feed, the net economic effect for producers of dropping AGPs was slightly positive.[75]

Results from a number of experiments by Dritz and his colleagues

---

74. WHO (2003, pp. 7–8, and 42).

75. Engster, Marvil, and Stewart-Brown (2002); and Graham, Boland, and Silbergeld (2007).

Figure 5-4   Sales of Active Ingredients of Antimicrobials for Food-
Producing Animals and Exports of Meat Products (SITC 01) in Denmark

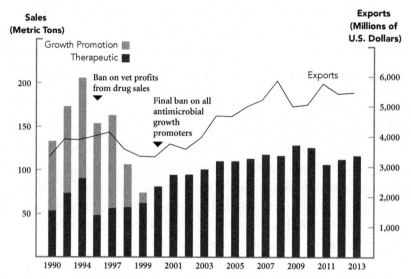

Sources: Antimicrobial sales: DANMAP, 2013 Report on the use of antimicrobial agents and occurrence of antimicrobial resistance in bacteria from food animals, food, and humans in Denmark Report; Exports: UN Comtrade (SITC Revision 1).

at Kansas State University similarly support the conclusions from other studies that the benefits of AGPs in pork production are limited with modern management systems. The KSU researchers found few benefits in older pigs, but some in younger pigs, which are more susceptible to disease.[76] Overall, in studies estimating the economic benefits of using antibiotics in swine, Kansas State researchers found that certain antibiotics in the feed of nursery pigs could raise producer incomes by $1 to $3 per pig.[77] Dritz told a reporter that new production methods are so effective in preventing disease that he tells pork producers "that most uses of antibiotics for growth promotion or feed efficiency really [do] not make sense anymore."[78]

76. The university reports the results of its research in annual Swine Day progress reports that are available on the Agriculture Sciences and Industry section of the Kansas State University website at http://www.asi.k-state.edu/species/swine/research-and-extension/ (accessed February 11, 2015).

77. Sotak and others (2010).

78. Charles (2013).

Figure 5-5   Sales of Active Ingredients of Antimicrobials for Food-Producing Animals and Exports of Meat Products (SITC 01) in the Netherlands

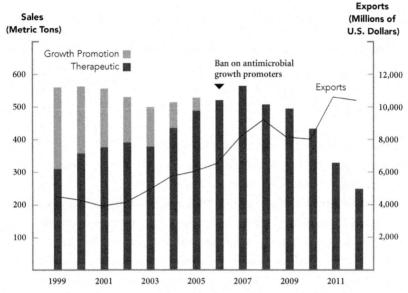

Sources: Antimicrobial sales: Monitoring of Antimicrobial Resistance and Antibiotic Usage in Animals in the Netherlands, 2012; Exports: United Nations Comtrade (SITC Revision 1).

To put things in perspective, in 1999 a U.S. National Research Council committee conducted a broad study of the benefits and risks of using antibiotics in food animals. As part of that study, the committee tried to assess the economic cost for livestock producers of a ban on the subtherapeutic use of antibiotics.[79] Like Wierup, who found that "progressive" farmers had better outcomes after Sweden banned AGPs, the committee pointed to U.S. studies finding that farmers with better management practices had less need for antibiotics and that these farmers could gain from a ban. The committee concluded:

> This raises the interesting possibility that a ban on subtherapeutic drug use would actually result in an economic incentive to improve animal care and could result in a more efficient industry in the long

79. As noted above, there is no consensus definition of what constitutes subtherapeutic or nontherapeutic use of antibiotics in farm animals. The NRC committee defined it as any use that is not to treat symptoms, so it includes disease prevention as well as growth promotion.

term. However, the process required to reach that point would be painful for those producers forced out of business.[80]

Given the heterogeneity among producers, the committee decided that trying to estimate an average cost for producers made little sense. They focused on the cost to consumers instead and concluded that banning subtherapeutic uses of antibiotics in chickens, turkeys, beef, and pork would cost between $0.34 and $0.75 per family per week.[81]

Simulations Suggest Limited Effects Globally

To get a sense of the impact globally and on developing countries, Laxminarayan and others estimate parameters for high and low growth responses to antimicrobial use from their review of the literature on AGPs in livestock production (discussed above). They then combine those parameters with estimates of antimicrobial consumption by country, from Van Boeckel and others to estimate the impact on livestock production of restricting antimicrobial use. They find that it would be relatively small in the aggregate, just 1.3 percent to 3 percent globally, with relatively larger negative effects in developing countries with less modern management systems. On the high end, in some developing countries like Sudan and Bangladesh, the loss in meat production might be 5 percent. The authors estimate that meat production might be lower by 1 percent to 3 percent in Brazil and China, and probably by around 1 percent in the United States.[82]

Thus, even in developing countries, the costs would be relatively modest. The authors calculate that the value of the total, global reduction in meat production might be $44 billion under the most pessimistic assumptions. And even if that figure is an order of magnitude too low, it would still be a tiny fraction of the $60 trillion in economic losses that the O'Neill review estimated could occur by 2050 if the world does not address antimicrobial resistance.[83]

80. NRC (1999, p. 181).

81. Based on the consumer price index for food, those figures would be roughly 50 percent higher today.

82. Laxminarayan, Van Boeckel, and Teillant (2015, pp. 27–33); and Van Boeckel and others (2015).

83. Review on Antimicrobial Resistance (2014).

Consumer Demand for Antibiotic-Free Meat

In assessing the net costs and benefits of antibiotic use in meat animals, it is useful to recall that the early moves to restrict AGPs in Sweden and Denmark were taken by or at the behest of livestock producers who were concerned that consumers would lose confidence in their product. Other producers, including in the United States, are also finding opportunities in the growing consumer demand for healthier food choices. The Perdue poultry company, after examining the results of the studies it commissioned showing a minimal impact from withdrawing AGPs, introduced a line of antibiotic-free chicken that now accounts for a third of the chicken it sells. Organic chicken is another 5 percent, while the rest receive medically important antibiotics only if needed to treat disease.[84]

In the United States, some large meat buyers, such as McDonald's and Chick-fil-A, have also adopted policies to reduce antibiotic use among their suppliers.[85] And at the end of 2014, the six largest U.S. school districts—Chicago, Dallas, Los Angeles, Miami-Dade, New York City, and Orlando County—announced that they would demand antibiotic-free chicken when they renew contracts with meat suppliers in coming years.[86] Thus, increasing consumer concerns about animal welfare and human health effects are forcing some producers to reconsider how they operate, even in the absence of government regulation.

MATCHING RHETORIC TO ACTION

The development of antibiotics was a huge boon to human health and the loss of this tool to widespread resistance would be enormously costly. Even minor infections or injuries could again become life-threatening,

---

84. Engster, Marvil, and Stewart-Brown (2002); and Sharpe (2014).

85. Some public health advocates criticized the McDonald's policy, which allowed continued prophylactic use, as too weak. See Elgin and Martin (2014). McDonald's website says that the policy is currently under review: www.aboutmcdonalds.com/content/dam /AboutMcDonalds/Sustainability/Sustainability%20Library/antibiotics_policy.pdf; for Chik-fil-A's policy, see the Chik-fil-A food ingredients website at www.chick-fil-a.com/ Food/Ingredients (accessed February 2, 2015).

86. See Polansek (2014).

while surgery and cancer treatment would be far riskier. Moreover, those costs would be borne disproportionately by the poor, and particularly by children who are most at risk from diarrheal and respiratory infections caused by bacteria. Developing country health systems are also already stretched thin, and they are least able to afford the more expensive second- and third-line antibiotics to which doctors must turn when older drugs fail.

The magnitude of the threat to human health from antibiotic use in farm animals remains uncertain. There is clear evidence that routine, subtherapeutic use of antibiotics increases the prevalence of resistant bacteria in farm animals, and that resistant bacteria can spread to humans through direct contact or via the food chain. What is not known is how often these problems result in antibiotic-resistant infections in humans. Even less is known about the risks of environmental exposure. The uncertainty is partly due to the large number of steps in the food chain and the complexity of the processes involved in the evolution of resistance. But the lack of knowledge is also due to the failure in most countries to systematically monitor antibiotic resistance and use. And, in the United States, we know very little about antibiotic use in livestock in part because of opposition to more detailed data collection from agro-industry.

So, although it is critical to collect and analyze detailed data on antibiotic use and resistance, doing so will take time and the magnitude of the risks to human health are high enough to justify precautionary steps to curtail the use of medically important antibiotics in farm animals in the meantime. Moreover, the mounting evidence that the costs to producers from reducing the use of antibiotics for growth promotion and disease prevention would not be large bolsters the case for action even as additional data are being collected.

As one of the world's largest meat producers and exporters, the United States needs to be a leader, not a laggard, in tackling this problem. President Obama's national action plan is a good first step but the provisions on livestock use and surveillance are too timid. The most recent FDA report on antibiotic use in farm animals is a step forward, but researchers also need to know how drugs are being used, in what doses, for how long, and in what species. The FDA recently launched a consultation process for how it might go about gathering more detailed data on livestock use, but it would not implement anything earlier than 2018. That is too long to wait to *begin* collecting and reporting more data. Congress also needs to adequately fund the elements in the action plan calling for expanding and improving the NARMS program on drug resistance in meat, as well as the on-farm-level data collection.[87]

Second, while the FDA actions to discourage AGP use are an important step forward, there are loopholes. The Obama national strategy addresses one of them with its proposal to fund educational programs to help livestock producers adapt their husbandry practices so that routine, prophylactic use of antibiotics is not necessary. In the meantime, FDA guidance allows farmers to continue using antibiotics to prevent disease and it relies on veterinarians to oversee that use. The experience in Denmark, as well as common sense, suggest that U.S. policies need to ensure that veterinarians do not profit from selling antibiotics or have financial ties with drug companies.

Finally, the problem is global. With many developing countries increasing meat and dairy production sharply, action to address the problem must also be global. This is a critical time to develop global policies to guide the prudent use of antibiotics in livestock, and to build capacity in developing countries to regulate that use. The first priority is the creation of harmonized surveillance systems in priority countries around the world. These systems need to be able to track antibiotic use and resistance in humans and animals. Improved surveillance is the key to being able to spot emerging resistance problems and respond effectively. Donors and the WHO are already ramping up financial and technical assistance to developing countries to create and strengthen disease surveillance in response to the Ebola epidemic. These efforts should be coordinated with efforts to expand and improve surveillance of antibiotic resistance and not remain in silos. The WHO and the OIE also need to provide platforms to publish surveillance and antibiotic use data in a harmonized format so that trouble spots can be identified and resources targeted to where they are most needed to slow the emergence of resistance.

---

87. See APUA's recommendations for improving NARMS the last time it was reauthorized on the Tufts University website at www.tufts.edu/med/apua/index_168_274705518.pdf (accessed February 11, 2015).

A global treaty setting targets for reduced use could be a powerful tool to encourage the development and adoption of alternatives to widespread use of antibiotics in livestock, just as the Montreal Protocol did for ozone-depleting substances in the 1990s.[88] In addition to targets for cuts in overall livestock use, such a treaty should move quickly to restrict the use in livestock of antibiotics that are critically important for human health. And, given the growing consensus that using antibiotics to promote growth in food animals is not a good use of a valuable resource, the treaty should ban this practice—immediately for advanced economies and as soon as possible in developing countries.

---

88. Review on Antimicrobial Resistance (2016); and Elliott, Kenny, and Madan (2017).

6

GRASPING OPPORTUNITIES FOR
AMERICAN LEADERSHIP

EVEN AS THE U.S. FEED THE FUTURE initiative helps to develop the agricultural sector in poor countries, a vibrant American agricultural sector is critical to global food security. The United States has abundant land, universities with top-notch agricultural research programs, and farmers with access to capital and the latest technologies. Those farmers will remain major producers and exporters of a range of commodities. Even with all those advantages, however, American farmers are vulnerable to the vagaries of weather and other unexpected supply or demand shocks. So there is a role for government to help farmers manage the risks that markets cannot.

But the U.S. government, like others around the world, supports the agriculture sector at levels far beyond what is socially optimal, or what other sectors receive. Unbeknownst to many, these subsidies go disproportionately to larger, richer farmers and only a few crops receive the bulk of the support—mainly grains, oilseeds, sugar, and dairy, rather than fruits and vegetables. The total value of that support is also difficult to know because it comes in a variety of forms, many of which are not as transparent as those in regularly debated farm bills. In addition, some support is the result of the government's *failure* to regulate the production of negative spillovers from agriculture.

Overall, U.S. policies affecting agriculture impose substantial costs on other Americans in their roles as consumers and taxpayers, as well as those downwind or downstream that suffer negative health or environmental consequences from farm activities. And, since the United States is a leading agricultural producer and exporter, its policies have a disproportionate effect on the rest of the world, particularly for the poorest countries that cannot afford to protect or subsidize their own farmers. The direct subsidies that Congress provides in the farm bill further depress global commodity prices when those prices are already low. They shield American producers from declining revenues and push the costs onto producers elsewhere. Moreover, some of the highest duties in the U.S. tariff schedule apply to agricultural products, including sugar, peanuts, and other commodities, that are key developing country exports.

While these traditional agricultural support policies generally focus on the supply side, biofuel policies support farmers by increasing demand for their output. This raises global prices and helps developing country producers. But U.S. and European Union policymakers ratcheted up their biofuel policies at the worst possible time, just as commodity prices were rising for other reasons. These policies were important contributors to the price spikes that roiled global markets in 2007–08. These agricultural and biofuel policies shield American farmers from low prices, but it is at the expense of increased uncertainty for poor producers and consumers in developing countries. Over the longer run, U.S. and other rich countries' trade-distorting agricultural policies distort decisions about what to produce and where, often to the detriment of developing countries.

Beyond these market effects, developing countries and their citizens are also the most vulnerable to the effects of global spillovers from U.S. agricultural policies, including climate change and antibiotic-resistant infections. A growing body of research shows that food-based biofuels are doing little to help mitigate climate change, and could be making it worse. U.S. policies to discourage farmers from routinely administering medically important antibiotics to healthy animals are both quite recent and relatively weak, despite the rapid spread of antibiotic-resistant infections.

Thus, across a range of areas, U.S. policy favors the narrow interests of the agriculture and related sectors over those of other American citizens and the poor and vulnerable in developing countries. The inability to overcome these entrenched interests also undermines U.S. leadership in the G8, G20, World Trade Organization, and other forums as the international community struggles to address the global issues of food security, climate change, and antibiotic resistance. Moreover, these policies remain entrenched despite the fact that farmers are a tiny share of the population and the average farm household income has been higher than that of the typical non-farm household in every year since 1996.[1] The top 10 percent of recipients accounted for 77 percent of total commodity payments between 1995 and 2014. In 2012, according to the Census of Agriculture, more than 60 percent of American farms received no government payments at all.[2] How has the system evolved this way?

GENERAL LESSONS FOR POLICYMAKERS

The experience with agricultural policies in high-income countries should be a cautionary tale for policymakers elsewhere. Each of the issue areas discussed in this book highlights different risks associated with policymaking that need careful attention at the front end to avoid problems later. One key lesson is that policymakers are almost always operating in an environment of incomplete information and with varying degrees of uncertainty, which underscores the need to design flexible policies that can be adapted to changing conditions. The examples in this book also underscore the need to build in off-ramps for policies that outlive their usefulness or turn out to have been based on faulty assumptions.

Sector-specific subsidy policies, like those for farmers, are often prone to capture for classic political economy reasons. The benefits are usually concentrated on a relatively small number of recipients, as documented

---

1. Zulauf (2013, p. 1).

2. The Environmental Working Group's Farm Subsidy Database is available at https://farm.ewg.org/index.php. Data on payment concentration are available at https://farm.ewg.org/progdetail.php?fips=00000&progcode=totalfarm&page=conc&regionname=the UnitedStates. The most recent (2012) Census of Agriculture is here available through the U.S. Department of Agriculture website at www.agcensus.usda.gov/Publications/2012/Full_Report/Volume_1,_Chapter_1_US/.

by the Environmental Working Group database cited above. The costs, in contrast, are spread across a large number of taxpayers or consumers who often do not even know that they are paying these costs. This makes it relatively easy for the beneficiaries to overcome collective action problems and organize to defend their subsidies. On the other side, opposition to agricultural subsidies is a decisive issue for very few voters and even fewer will care enough to make campaign contributions related to the issue. It has been eight decades since the Great Depression and Dust Bowl devastated many rural households, and American farmers today are an export powerhouse. Yet American agriculture continues to receive an array of taxpayer-funded subsidies and other support beyond what can be justified by market failures.

In the case of biofuels, the United States, the EU, and other countries ramped up support at a time when oil prices were expected to stay high and research suggested that renewable fuels were the quickest, easiest way to reduce transportation-related greenhouse gas emissions. Not long after, fracking technology opened up substantial new sources of oil and gas in the United States, growth slowed in China and other emerging markets, and the price of oil plummeted. At the same time, new economic and scientific research has continued to raise more questions about the benefits of food-based biofuels in the battle against climate change. But, because Congress did not anticipate that conditions might change and designed a biofuels mandate that is relatively rigid, the Environmental Protection Agency is struggling to implement a policy that no longer makes sense.

The final example from this book presents the extremely complex issue of antibiotic resistance and the links between use of antibiotics in livestock and effects on human health. We know that the routine use of low doses of antibiotics to promote growth and prevent disease in healthy farm animals contributes to the pool of antibiotic-resistant bacteria, and that some of these bacteria can spread to humans and cause infections. Zoonotic bacteria also can pass the resistance gene to other bacteria that can infect humans. But scientists do not understand exactly how the channels work, or how often humans might suffer or die from infections that resist treatment. The dilemma here is determining how much of a potential loss in agricultural productivity is acceptable to avoid the large but uncertain risk of losing antibiotics as an effective treatment. To add to the difficulties, however, there is also uncertainty about the magnitude of the potential losses to livestock producers from withdrawing antibiotic growth promoters.

Developing countries are unlikely to adopt "do as I say, not as I do" advice from American, or any other, policymakers. But hopefully they are paying attention to how U.S. and other advanced country agricultural policies have gone wrong. The optimal response in most situations will be to provide public support for agriculture only for public goods or to overcome market failures. There is an ample agenda here in most countries, including infrastructure; protection of plant, animal, and human health; and research and development to improve productivity. However, very few countries have managed to avoid the trap of continuing and expanding agricultural subsidies far beyond what is socially optimal once they are in place.

Among the key principles for managing the costs of agricultural policies that emerge from the case studies here are transparency, market orientation, the willingness to accept sunk costs and move on, and the importance of learning and flexibility. Transparency often is insufficient to prevent special interests from capturing a policy, but it is still a first step toward reform by making it clear who is getting what and who is paying for it. So, for example, simple ad valorem tariffs are preferable to other forms of tariffs or quantitative restrictions where the costs to consumers are less obvious. Policies that are relatively more market-oriented, such as using a moving average rather than a fixed reference price to calculate subsidy payments to farmers, will be less distorting of global markets and may be less costly over time to taxpayers.

In some cases, policymakers base decisions on assumptions that turn out to be wrong, as with biofuels. In this case, it is relatively easy for farmers to revert to selling corn or soybeans for feed rather than biofuels, though perhaps at a lower average price. But biofuel producers have invested millions of dollars in processing facilities with the expectation that there will be a demand for so many billion gallons of ethanol every year. And those plants are not easily adapted to alternative uses if the government changes its mind about the energy independence or environmental benefits of biofuels.

In this case, governments have three options for dealing with these "stranded assets." They can try to reverse the policy with no compensation, but that will generate strong political opposition from those who invested under the policy in good faith. It could also undermine the use of similar incentives in the future to support policies that would be socially optimal. At the other extreme, policymakers can "buy out" beneficiaries, as the United States did with production allotments for peanut and to-bacco growers that were used to control supplies and prop up prices. Or, policymakers can freeze the policy in place, as the EU did with its biofuel mandate.

Finally, where there is a great deal of uncertainty about either the costs or benefits of a particular policy, as with antibiotic resistance, policymak-ers should emphasize learning and flexibility. The first priorities should be to increase efforts to collect data and to support research to understand the problem. If the potential risks are high, policymakers may not want to wait for new information to become available. But any policies they introduce should include speed bumps and exit ramps so they can make adjustments if the policies turn out to be unnecessary or in the wrong direction. So, as with the Montreal Protocol on Ozone Depleting Sub-stances, governments could start with relatively modest targets for re-ducing antibiotic use in livestock and design a mechanism to adjust the targets up or down as new information on the effects of antibiotic use becomes available. They could also prioritize options that would be useful whatever the results of new research, such as investments in vaccines or other alternatives to antibiotic use in livestock.

STEPS TOWARD A BETTER FARM POLICY
FOR AMERICANS AND THE WORLD

The next U.S. farm bill debate in 2017–18 is likely to be a challenge for reformers. With commodity prices down, farm groups and their repre-sentatives in Congress argue that the last farm bill left farmers too vul-nerable. Wholesale changes to reduce subsidies or to agree to substantial reductions in WTO trade barriers thus seem unlikely in the short run. But mounting opposition to parts of the farm bill, as well as the ethanol mandate, and growing urgency around the problem of antibiotic-resistant bacteria provide the foundation for at least some progress in each of these areas. This section provides a brief summary of key recommendations from the earlier chapters for feasible, short-run reforms. The idea of these reforms is not to eliminate support for farmers entirely. Rather, the aim is to reduce the costs imposed on others, particularly the poor and vulnerable around the world, and to channel more support to the creation of public goods, such as infrastructure and scientific research and development.

Budget pressures continue to be a problem for farm bill advocates and the sharp increase in crop insurance subsidies is a fat target. These subsidies, which now cover more than 60 percent of the average premium for buying crop insurance, affect decisions about both about what to produce and how much. Reducing them would benefit American taxpayers as well as producers in developing countries. The sugar program, by contrast, was designed to be off budget and is one of the most trade-distorting as a result. It uses import and domestic supply controls to prop up prices for domestic producers, but it is coming under increasing pressures from a number of directions. A buyout of sugar producers, or at least those in environmentally sensitive areas of Florida and other states, would reduce the costs of the program in the long run and, in conjunction with elimination of restrictions on imports, would open important new export opportunities for developing countries.

Food aid is another area that is overdue for reform. The challenges associated with delivering in-kind food aid in Syria and other conflict areas highlight the degree to which U.S. food aid is outmoded, inefficient, and costly. The current system serves mainly to support a handful of jobs in the U.S. shipping industry while the share of total U.S. farm production that goes to food aid is trivial. U.S. commodity groups would lose little and could get a big reputational boost by joining the forces of reform and accepting the elimination of the requirements to procure food aid in the United States and ship it on U.S.-flagged ships.

Beyond the farm bill, the flaws in the policy requiring the blending of biofuels in gasoline and diesel become more obvious all the time. Congress vastly overestimated the potential for advanced, cellulosic biofuels to quickly develop and underestimated the degree to which high prices and fuel efficiency standards could reduce gasoline demand. What is difficult to understand is why Congress chose to expand the mandate even as corn, soybean, and other food prices were rising sharply in late 2007. The

EPA, besieged by costly lawsuits, has struggled to implement the mandate despite technological constraints on blending ever higher amounts of ethanol in gasoline, and the shortfalls in cellulosic biofuel supplies. Rather than adding more subsidies for infrastructure to expand the market for corn-based ethanol in order to meet the mandate, Congress should change the mandate. If it is politically impossible to eliminate the mandate, Congress should make it easier to adapt to changing conditions and cap the food-based portion at roughly the current level of 10 percent of consumption—a decision that would stem the program's economic and environmental costs and have minimal costs for current investors because ethanol would still be in demand as a gasoline additive under Clean Air Act regulations.

Addressing the livestock contribution to antibiotic resistance is a tough problem for policymakers because the potential costs of not acting are enormous but the science around the risks for human health is still uncertain. Thus, it is vital to support data collection and reporting, and to do so in a way that the data are comparable across countries. Congress needs to provide adequate funding for this. Second, the U.S. National Action Plan to Combat Antibiotic-Resistant Bacteria gives veterinarians a crucial role in ensuring that antibiotic use in livestock is done responsibly. Currently, however, veterinarians do not have to report any financial ties to pharmaceutical companies, as medical doctors are required to do. Regulators need to take steps to ensure that veterinarians do not have financial incentives to prescribe antibiotics that might conflict with public health priorities. At a minimum they should have to report any financial ties to the drug industry, just as human doctors do. Finally, the cross-border nature of the drug resistance problems makes global cooperation an imperative in this area.

THE ROLE OF GLOBAL COOPERATION

Agricultural policy reforms will not happen in the absence of domestic pressures, but global cooperation can help. International demands can reinforce pressures at home, or provide an excuse for national leaders to do something they would like to do but for which they lack domestic support—*gaiatsu*, as the Japanese call it, literally "foreign pressure." International rules can also help to lock in reforms once adopted. And, in the case of global public goods, cooperation is essential for success.

Of the cases examined in this book, international cooperation could help to discipline beggar-thy-neighbor agricultural subsidy policies. But the history suggests it may be better at locking in domestic reforms than stimulating new ones. International cooperation will be critical in the struggle to stem antibiotic resistance since dangerous infections do not respect borders. The perceived commercial competition effects make an international approach particularly important in the area of agricultural use. With respect to biofuels policies, the broader issue of climate change that they were nominally supposed to address remains centrally on the international agenda. But for the narrower issue of biofuels, the costs of implementing support policies have become so obvious that international cooperation might not be necessary to achieve reform. Many developing countries are allowing targets to go unmet because of the costs. The EU, concerned about both global and local costs, opted to cap its support more or less where it is, thus avoiding the stranding of assets but not encouraging much additional growth. The United States should follow a similar path, implicitly if not explicitly.

In sum, hunger, poverty, climate change, and the spread of drug-resistant superbugs are global problems that will ultimately require global solutions. But U.S. policy looms large, and domestic reform would contribute to solving the global challenges, while saving American taxpayers money, improving their health, and promoting U.S. national security. These are not battles where the United States can sit on the sidelines.

Appendix A

THOUGH LARGELY HIDDEN, U.S. BIOFUEL
POLICY CONTRIBUTES TO PALM OIL DEMAND

IN CONTRAST TO EUROPE, the United States relies less on diesel for transportation fuel and biodiesel is a far smaller share of that diesel consumption. Soybean oil is the principal feedstock for biodiesel in the United States and, by 2011, biodiesel demand was diverting around a quarter of U.S. soybean oil production from other uses.[1] But these policies are also contributing to demand for palm oil, both as a feedstock and as a substitute for soybean oil in food uses. Though systematic data on palm oil use in biodiesel are not available, a rough estimate suggests that, in 2013, U.S. demand for palm oil as a biodiesel feedstock was about a quarter of that in the EU (appendix table A-1).

Initially, the U.S. Congress did not include targets for biodiesel in the RFS passed in 2005. But it had approved a $1 per gallon tax credit for blenders using biodiesel in 2004, and demand surged the next year when disruptions to Gulf coast refineries from Hurricane Katrina disrupted supplies of conventional fuels.[2] Congress then added biodiesel as a sepa-

1. USDA reports on the supply and use of oilseeds, including soybean oil, in the Economic Research Service's "Oil Crops Yearbook" at www.ers.usda.gov/data-products/oil-crops-yearbook.aspx.

2. Schnepf (2013, pp. 10 and 21).

Appendix Table A-1　　Comparing Palm Oil Use for Biodiesel
in the United States and European Union, 2013

	United States	European Union
Palm oil imports used as feedstocks by domestic industry	632m lbs. (EIA) = 287k MT = 326m liters	1,410k MT (USDA) = 1,602m liters
Biodiesel imports from Indonesia, Malaysia	253k MT (USITC) = 287m liters	602k MT (Comtrade) = 684m liters[a]
Palm oil content in biodiesel (at mid-range yield)	298k MT	712k MT
Total effective palm oil	585k MT	2,122k MT
U.S., EU biodiesel share in global palm oil exports (including biodiesel exports from Indonesia, Malaysia)	6.7%	

Sources: UN Comtrade and author's calculations.

Notes: MT biodiesel = 1,136 liters; MT palm oil = 1,087 liters; MT palm oil yields 905–1,016 liters of biodiesel (83.3% to 93.5%); conversion factors from EU 2013; Indonesia 2013 GAIN reports; World imports palm oil, 2013 = 39m MT; World imports biodiesel from Indonesia, Malaysia = 1.2m MT = 1,363m liters = 1.4m MT of palm oil as feedstock.

a. This figure is down about a third from the 2012 level, before the EU imposed import duties; estimates of EU use of palm oil as a feedstock in its own industry show a similar increase.

rate category in the revised Renewable Fuel Mandate in 2008, which the EPA began implementing in 2010. The EPA ultimately concluded that palm oil was not an eligible feedstock under the mandate because greenhouse gas emissions from indirect land use change would keep palm oil biodiesel below the 50 percent net emissions reduction threshold.[3]

Despite the EPA decision, the $1 per gallon tax credit for blending biodiesel is under a separate law and palm oil biodiesel has been eligible

3. EPA (2011).

to collect it when blended with regular diesel.[4] With a large enough gap between palm and soy oil prices, it could be profitable to import palm oil biodiesel. Any biodiesel produced in the United States using palm oil as a feedstock would also be eligible for the tax credit, but generally would not be counted under the mandate.[5] For 2013, the U.S. International Trade Commission (USITC) reports that the United States imported 253,000 metric tons (MT) of biodiesel from Indonesia (none from Malaysia). The USITC database shows no U.S. imports of biodiesel from Indonesia (or Malaysia) in 2012 and only 86,000 MT through August 2014, periods when the tax credit had lapsed. Since palm oil biodiesel cannot be counted against the RFS2 mandate, blenders may be exporting that fuel and then importing eligible biodiesel to fill the mandate. The Energy Information Agency's Monthly Energy Review shows some circular trade in biodiesel in 2013, with 188 million gallons exported and 315 million gallons imported.

Overall, U.S. imports of palm oil quintupled from around 0.2 million MT in the early 2000s to 1 million MT in the late 2000s, and 1.4 million MT in 2013. In addition to some use as a biodiesel feedstock, concerns about the health risks of trans fats that arose in the mid-2000s led food companies to substitute palm oil for hydrogenated oils in some products. Palm oil is also likely substituting in other food uses for soybean oil that is more expensive because of biofuel demand. Unfortunately, it is difficult from the publicly available data to determine exactly how much of the imported palm oil is for biodiesel and how much is for food or other uses. U.S. government statistical agencies cannot report data that might have the effect of disclosing individual company data. Thus, Bureau of the Census data, which typically have the most detail, are spotty at best. The Energy Information Agency has been reporting monthly on biodiesel

4. Yacobucci and Bracmort (2010, p. 2, fn. 7).

5. Irwin (2014) notes that the only two recent periods of profitability for biodiesel producers were in 2011 and 2013 when blenders increased demand to take advantage of the tax credit before it expired. The International Council on Clean Transportation (ICCT) also suggests that some palm oil biodiesel from grandfathered facilities (those in existence prior to the EISA changes to the mandate in 2008) might be eligible under RFS2 as well; see Stephanie Searle, "An Unexpected Tax Bill for Imported Palm Oil Biodiesel," ICCT, January 25, 2015, www.theicct.org/blogs/staff/unexpected-tax-bill-for-imported-palm-oil-biodiesel.

production and feedstocks since 2009. That series indicates that palm oil was used as a feedstock in all but three of those months. And, in 2013, there was apparently enough activity from different companies that the agency was able to report that 632 million pounds (287,000 MT) of palm oil were used in the production of biodiesel.[6] The table shows estimates of the American use of palm oil for biodiesel and compares it to that in the EU.

Unless there is a supply shock affecting soybean production that opens a relatively large gap between soybean oil and palm oil prices, the tax credit is the only reason for palm oil biodiesel to be in the U.S. market. The tax credit has been off and on because of budget constraints, but each time it expired, Congress reinstated it with retroactive application.

6. The Monthly Biodiesel Production Report is available on the Energy Information Agency website at www.eia.gov/biofuels/biodiesel/production/ (accessed November 18, 2014).

Appendix B

LIVESTOCK AND CLIMATE CHANGE

GREENHOUSE GAS EMISSIONS ARE ANOTHER way in which livestock contributes to global public bads. Heat-trapping gases, which lead to climate change, are released along all stages of the livestock supply chain, from animal rearing to packaging and refrigeration of meat products. Livestock's contribution to emissions can be categorized along direct and indirect pathways.[1] Methane is directly released as a by-product of digestive fermentation in ruminant animals (cattle, buffalo, sheep, and goats), while manure creates nitrous oxide emissions. Fertilizer use, including manure, to grow animal feed is an important indirect pathway. Energy use in processing, packaging, storing, and transporting meat products also produces carbon dioxide. In addition, livestock indirectly contributes to climate change through changes in land use patterns. When land areas, and especially forests, are cleared for pasture or used to grow feed crops, large amounts of carbon can be added to the atmosphere.

These pathways are well understood, and yet it is difficult to quantify them. Emissions from livestock overlap with multiple sectors, including agriculture, energy, transport, and land use and forestry.[2] This overlap

1. FAO (2013).
2. FAO (2006, p. 112).

makes it especially challenging to account for the indirect emissions. In 2005, the Intergovernmental Panel on Climate Change reported that the agriculture sector contributes 13.5 percent, or 6.6 of the 49 gigatons of CO_2 equivalent from human-caused emissions globally per year. A 2005 World Resources Institute report provided a more detailed breakdown showing that livestock and manure management account for approximately 40 percent of emissions within agriculture, or 5.1 percent of total global emissions. However, these estimates only account for direct emissions.[3]

More recently, the UN Food and Agriculture Organization conducted a life-cycle analysis to provide a more comprehensive picture of livestock's role in climate change. The FAO estimates that livestock supply chains directly and indirectly contribute 7 gigatons of CO_2 equivalent per year, or 14.5 percent of global human-induced emissions.[4] Livestock production (enteric fermentation as well as manure storage and processing) accounts for 50 percent, with feed production contributing 47 percent, and post-farm transport and processing responsible for the remaining 3 percent. However, due to differences in methodology and accounting for indirect emissions across multiple sectors, it is not possible to directly compare data from various sources.

Despite the challenges underlying quantitative estimates, the evidence suggests that emissions along the livestock supply chain constitute a significant contribution to GHG emissions. It is precisely because of livestock's large contribution that sustainable practices can serve as an important mitigation and adaptation strategy. In addition to changes in meat production systems, consumption patterns will also need to shift in the face of growing climate change concerns.

3. Baumert and others (2005, p. 6).
4. FAO (2013, p. 15).

REFERENCES

Aarestrup, F. M. 2012. "Sustainable Farming: Get Pigs Off Antibiotics." *Nature* 486 (June 28), pp. 465–66.

Aarestrup, F. M., V. F. Jensen, H.-D. Emorg, E. Jacobsen, and H. C. Wegener. 2010. "Changes in the Use of Antimicrobials and the Effects on Productivity of Swine Farms in Denmark." *American Journal of Veterinary Research* 71, issue 7 (July), pp. 726–33.

Abbott, P. C. 2013. "Biofuels, Binding Constraints and Agricultural Commodity Price Volatility," Working Paper 18873 (Cambridge, Mass.: National Bureau of Economic Research), www.nber.org/papers/w18873.

Abbott, P. C., C. Hurt, and W. E. Tyner. 2008. "What's Driving Food Prices?" Oak Brook, Ill.: Farm Foundation.

Achten, W. M. J., and L. V. Verchot. 2011. "Implications of Biodiesel-Induced Land-Use Changes for CO_2 Emissions: Cast Studies in Tropical America, Africa, and Southeast Asia." *Ecology and Society* 16, no. 4, www.ecologyand-society.org/vol16/iss4/art14/.

Agrosynergie. 2011. *Evaluation of CAP Measures Applied to the Sugar Sector.* Final Report to DG Agriculture and Rural Development, European Commission. December.

Aksoy, M. A., and J. C. Beghin. 2005. "Introduction and Overview," in *Global Agricultural Trade and Developing Countries*, edited by M. A. Aksoy and John C. Beghin (World Bank), pp. 1–13.

Aksoy, M. A., and B. Hoekman, eds. 2010. "Food Prices and Rural Poverty" (Washington, D.C.: World Bank and Centre for Economic Policy Research).

Aksoy, M. A., and A. Isik-Dikmelik. 2010. "Are Low Food Prices Pro-Poor? Net Food Buyers and Sellers in Low-Income Countries," in *Food Prices and Rural Poverty*, edited by M. Aksoy and B. Hoekman (Washington, D.C.: World Bank and Centre for Economic Policy Research), pp. 113–38.

Alexandratos, N., and J. Bruinsma. 2012. "World Agriculture towards 2030/2050: The 2012 Revision," ESA Working Paper 12-03 (Rome: Food and Agriculture Organization of the United Nations).

Amezaga, J. M., S. L. Boyes, and J. A. Harrison. 2010. "Biofuels Policy in the European Union." Paper presented at the 7th International Biofuels Conference, New Delhi, Winrock International India.

Anderson, K., G. Rausser, and J. Swinnen. 2013. "Political Economy of Public Policies: Insights from Distortions to Agricultural and Food Markets," Policy Research Working Paper 6433 (World Bank).

Animal Health Institute. 2001. "2000–2001 Antibiotic Sales Member Survey." Washington, D.C. [Data cited in "Survey Shows Decline in Antibiotic Use in Animals," *Prnewswire.com*, September 29, 2002, www.prnewswire.com/news-releases/survey-shows-decline-in-antibiotic-use-in-animals-decrease-from-1999-to-2001-despite-increased-meat-production-75959657.html.

———. 2004. "2003 Antibiotic Sales Member Survey." Washington, D.C. [Data cited in "AHI Survey Shows Decline in Volume of Antibiotics Used." *Feedstuffs*, October 11, 2004, accessed through HighBeam Research, www.highbeam.com/doc/1G1-123636146.html.

———. 2008. "2007 Antibiotics Sales: Sales of Disease Fighting Animal Medicines Rise." AHI Press Release. Washington, D.C., November 14.

Babcock, B. 2011. "The Impact of Ethanol and Ethanol Subsidies on Corn Prices: Revisiting History." CARD Policy Brief 11-PB 5 (Ames, Iowa: Iowa State University, Center for Agricultural and Rural Development, April).

Babcock, B., and N. Paulson. 2012. "Potential Impact of Proposed 2012 Farm Bill Commodity Programs on Developing Countries," ICTSD Issue Paper No. 45 (Geneva: International Center for Trade and Sustainable Development).

Baffes, J. 2013. "A Framework for Analyzing the Interplay among Food, Fuels, and Biofuels." *Global Food Security* 2, no. 2 (July), pp. 110–16.

Bageant, E., C. Barrett, and E. C. Lentz. 2010. "Food Aid and Agricultural Cargo Preference." *Applied Economics Perspectives and Policy* 32, no. 4 (December), pp. 624–41.

Barnett, B., K. Coble, and S. Mercier. 2016. "Public and Private Roles in Agricultural Risk Transfer," in *Four Papers on the U.S. Federal Crop Insurance Program* (Washington, D.C.: Agree), pp. 27–70.

Baumert, K., T. Herzog, and J. Pershing. 2005. "Navigating the Numbers: Greenhouse Gas Data and International Climate Policy" (Washington, D.C.: World Resources Institute).

Beinecke, F. 2012. "The Failure of the FDA: Why We're Still Using Antibiotics on Livestock." *The Atlantic* (January 17), www.theatlantic.com/health/archive/2012/01/the-failure-of-the-fda-why-were-still-using-antibiotics-on-livestock/251442/.

Blustein, P. 2008. "The Nine-Day Misadventure of the Most Favored Nations: How the WTO's Doha Round Negotiations Went Awry in July 2008," Brookings Institution, December 5, www.brookings.edu/~/media/Research/Files/Articles/2008/12/05-trade-blustein/1205_trade_blustein.PDF.

Bureau, J.-C., D. Laborde, and D. Orden. 2013. "US and EU Farm Policies: The Subsidy Habit," in *2012 Global Food Policy Report* (Washington, D.C.: International Food Policy Research Institute), pp. 58–67.

Busch, J., and K. Ferretti-Gallon. 2014a. "Stopping Deforestation: What Works and What Doesn't," CGD Brief (Washington, D.C.: Center for Global Development).

———. 2014b. "What Drives Deforestation and What Stops It? A Meta-Analysis of Spatially Explicit Econometric Studies," Working Paper No. 361 (Washington, D.C.: Center for Global Development).

Campenhout, V. B., K. Pauw, and N. Minot. 2013. "The Impact of Food Prices Shocks in Uganda: First-Order versus Long-Run Effects," Discussion Paper 1284 (Washington, D.C.: International Food Policy Research Institute).

Casinge, E. 2015. "Parliament Rubber Stamps EU Biofuels Reform Amid Final Controversy." EurActiv.com, April 29, www.euractiv.com/sections/transport/parliament-rubber-stamps-eu-biofuels-reform-amid-final-controversy-314196.

Center for a Livable Future. 2013. "Industrial Food Animal Production in America: Examining the Impact of the Pew Commission's Priority Recommendations" (Baltimore: Johns Hopkins University).

Centers for Disease Control and Prevention (CDC). 2013. "Antibiotic Resistance Threats in the United States, 2013." Atlanta.

CGD Working Group on Global Trade Preference Reform. 2010. *Open Markets for the Poorest Countries: Trade Preferences That Work.* Final Working Group Report (Washington, D.C.: Center for Global Development).

Charles, D. 2013. "Why Are Pig Farmers Still Using Growth-Promoting Drugs?" *The Salt* (November 1) (Washington, D.C.: National Public Radio), www.npr.org/sections/thesalt/2013/11/04/241603861/why-are-pig-farmers-still-using-growth-promoting-drugs.

Chum, H., and others. 2011. "Bioenergy," in *IPCC Special Report on Renewable Energy Sources and Climate Change Mitigation* (Cambridge University Press), pp. 209–332.

Cline, W. 2007. "Global Warming and Agriculture: Impact Estimates by Country" (Washington, D.C.: Center for Global Development).

Cogliani, C., H. Goossens, and C. Greko. 2011. "Restricting Antimicrobial Use in Food Animals: Lessons from Europe." *Microbe Magazine*.6, issue 6 (June), pp. 274–79.

Collins, K. 2008. "The Role of Biofuels and Other Factors in Increasing Farm and

Food Prices: A Review of Recent Developments with a Focus on Feed Grain Markets and Market Prospects." Supporting material for a review conducted by Kraft Foods Global, Inc., www.foodbeforefuel.org/facts/studies/role-bio fuels-and-other-factors-increasing-farm-andfood-prices.

Condon, N., H. Klemick, and A. Wolverton. 2013. "Impacts of Ethanol Policy on Corn Prices: A Review and Meta-Analysis of Recent Evidence," Working Paper 13-05 (Washington, D.C.: National Center for Environmental Economics, U.S. Environmental Protection Agency).

Congressional Budget Office (CBO). 2014. "The Renewable Fuel Standard: Issues for 2014 and Beyond." Washington, D.C.

———. 2016. "CBO's March 2016 Baseline for Farm Programs." Washington, D.C., March 24.

Congressional Research Service. 2014. "The 2014 Farm Bill (P.L. 133-79): Summary and Side-by-Side," CRS Report R43076 (Washington, D.C.).

Danish Integrated Antimicrobial Resistance Monitoring and Research Programme (DANMAP). 2000. "Consumption of Antimicrobial Agents and Occurrence of Antimicrobial Resistance in Bacteria from Food Animals, Foods and Humans in Denmark." Copenhagen.

Dawe, D., and T. Slayton. 2010. "The World Rice Market Crisis of 2007–08," in *The Rice Crisis*, edited by D. Dawe (London: Earthscan), pp. 15–28.

Deaton, A. 1989. "Household Survey Data and Pricing Policies in Developing Countries." *World Bank Economic Review* 3, no. 2 (May 31).

DeCicco, J., and R. Krishnan. 2015. *Annual Basis Carbon (ABC) Analysis of Biofuel Production at the Facility Level* (Ann Arbor: University of Michigan Energy Institute).

De Gorter, H., D. Drabik, and D. R. Just. 2013. "How Biofuels Policies Affect the Level of Grains and Oilseed Prices: Theory, Models and Evidence." *Global Food Security* 2, no. 2 (July), pp. 82–88.

———. 2015. *Economics of Biofuel Policies: Impacts on Price Volatility in Grain and Oilseed Markets* (Palgrave Macmillan).

De Hoyos, R. E., and D. Medvedev. 2009. "Poverty Effects of Higher Food Prices: A Global Perspective," Policy Research Working Paper no. 4887 (Washington, D.C.: World Bank).

DTB Associates, LLP. 2013. "Agricultural Subsidies in Key Developing Countries." Washington, D.C.

Dutil, L., and others. 2010. "Ceftiofur Resistance in Salmonella Enteric Serovar Heidelberg from Chicken Meat and Humans, Canada." *Emerging Infectious Diseases* 16, no. 1 (January), pp. 48–54, doi:10.3201/eid1601.090729.

Elgin, B., and A. Martin. 2014. "Animal Antibiotics: FDA Rules Criticized as Weak as McDonald's." *Bloomberg*, January 2, www.bloomberg.com/news/articles /2014-01-02/animal-antibiotics-fda-rules-criticized-as-weak-as-mcdonalds.

Elliott, K. A. 2006. "Delivering on Doha: Farm Trade and the Poor" (Washington, D.C.: Center for Global Development and Peterson Institute for International Economics).

———. 2008. "Biofuels and the Food Price Crisis: A Survey of the Issues," CGD Working Paper 151 (Washington, D.C.: Center for Global Development).

———. 2014. "AGOA's Final Frontier: Removing US Farm Trade Barriers," CGD Notes (Washington, D.C.: Center for Global Development).

———. 2015a. "Food Security in Developing Countries: Is There a Role for the WTO?," CGD Essay (Washington, D.C.: Center for Global Development).

———. 2015b. "Biofuel Policies: Fuel versus Food, Forests, and Climate," CGD Policy Paper 051 (Washington, D.C.: Center for Global Development).

———. 2016. "How Much 'Mega' in the Mega-Regional TPP and TTIP: Implications for Developing Countries," CGD Policy Paper 079 (Washington, D.C.: Center for Global Development).

Elliott, K. A., and W. McKitterick. 2013. "Food Aid for the 21st Century: Saving More Money, Time, and Lives," CGD Brief (Washington, D.C.: Center for Global Development).

Elliott, K. A., C. Kenny, and J. Madan. 2017. "A Global Treaty to Reduce Antimicrobial Use in Livestock," CGD Policy Paper 099 (Washington, D.C.: Center for Global Development).

Emborg, H.-D., and others. 2001. "The Effect of Discontinuing the Use of Antimicrobial Growth Promoters on the Productivity in the Danish Broiler Production." *Preventive Veterinary Medicine* 50, issue 1–2 (July 19), pp. 53–70.

Energy Information Administration. 2012. "Biofuels Issues and Trends" (Washington, DC: U.S. Department of Energy).

Engster, H. M., D. Marvil, and B. Stewart-Brown. 2002. "The Effect of Withdrawing Growth Promoting Antibiotics from Broiler Chickens: A Long-Term Commercial Industry Study." *Journal of Applied Poultry Research* 11, no. 4 (Winter), pp. 431–36.

European Commission. 2012. "Impact Assessment: Accompanying the Document Proposal for a Directive of the European Parliament and of the Council Amending Directive 98/70/EC Relating to the Quality of Petrol and Diesel Fuels and Amending Directive 2009/28/EC on the Promotion of the Use of Energy from Renewable Sources." Commission Staff Working Document. SWD (2012) 343 final. Brussels.

———. 2013. "Memo: CAP Reform—An Explanation of the Main Elements." MEMO/13/621. Brussels, June 26.

———. 2014a. "A Policy Framework for Climate and Energy in the Period from 2020 to 2030." Communication from the Commission to the European Parliament, the Council, the European Economic and Social Committee and the Committee of the Regions. COM (2014) 15 final. Brussels, January 22.

———. 2014b. "Guidelines on State Aid for Environmental Protection and Energy 2014–2020." Communication from the Commission. *Official Journal of the European Union,* 2014/C 200/01. Brussels, June 28.

European Medicines Agency (EMA). 2014. *Sales of Veterinary Antimicrobial Agents in 26 EU/EEA Countries in 2012.* European Surveillance of Veterinary Antimicrobial Consumption (EVSAC), Fourth Edition Report.

European Parliament. 2012. "Comparative Analysis of Agricultural Support within the Major Agricultural Trading Nations," study prepared for the Committee on Agriculture and Rural Development by Policy Department B: Structural and Cohesion Policies, Directorate General for Internal Policies, Study IP/B/AGRI/IC/2011-068. Brussels, May.

European Union (EU). 2003. "Directive 2003/30/EC of the European Parliament and of the Council of 8 May 2003 on the Promotion of the Use of Biofuels or Other Renewable Fuels for Transport." *Official Journal of the European Union,* L 123/42, May 17.

Executive Office of the President. 2014. "National Strategy for Combating Antibiotic Resistant Bacteria" (Washington, D.C.: White House).

Fargione, J., and others. 2008. "Land Clearing and the Biofuel Carbon Debt." *Science* 319 (2008), pp. 1235–38.

Feed the Future. 2015. *Achieving Impact: Leadership and Partnership to Feed the Future.* Washington, D.C.

Flach, B., and others. 2011, 2013, and 2014. "EU: Biofuels Annual," GAIN Report NL1013, NL3034, and NL4025 (Washington, D.C.: U.S. Foreign Agricultural Service, Global Agricultural Information Network, various issues).

Follet, G. 2000. "Antibiotic Resistance in the EU—Science, Politics, and Policy." *AgBioForum* 3, issue 2 & 3, pp. 148–55.

Food and Agriculture Organization of the United Nations (FAO). 2006. *Livestock's Long Shadow: Environmental Issues and Options.* Rome.

———. 2009. *The State of Agricultural Commodity Markets: High Food Prices and the Food Crisis—Experiences and Lessons Learned.* Rome.

———. 2012a. *The State of Food and Agriculture: Investing in Agriculture for a Better Future.* Rome.

———. 2012b. *World Agriculture Towards 2030/2050* (2012 rev.), "Summary." Rome.

———. 2013. *Tackling Climate Change through Livestock: A Global Assessment of Emissions and Mitigation Opportunities.* Rome.

FAO, World Health Organization (WHO), and World Organization for Animal Health (OIE). 2007. "Expert Meeting on Critically Important Antimicrobials." Report of the FAO/WHO/OIE Expert Meeting, Rome, November 26–30.

Food and Drug Administration (FDA) and Department of Health and Human Services. 2014. "Antimicrobials Sold or Distributed for Use in Food-Producing Animals, 2012." Summary Report. Silver Spring, Md.

Gelb, A., and A. Diofasi. 2015. "What Determines Purchasing Power Exchange Rates?" CGD Working Paper 416 (Washington, D.C.: Center for Global Development).

Gerasimchuk, I., R. Bridle, C. Beaton, and C. Charles. 2012. *State of Play on Biofuel Subsidies: Are Policies Ready to Shift?* Global Subsidies Initiative Research Report (Geneva: International Institute for Sustainable Development, June).

Glauber, J. W. 2016a. "After Nairobi: Public Stockholding for Food Security," in *Evaluating Nairobi: What Does the Outcome Mean for Trade in Food and Farm Goods?*, edited by J. Hepburn and C. Bellmann (Geneva: International Centre for Trade and Sustainable Development), pp. 69–80.

———. 2016b. "Unfinished Business in Agricultural Trade Liberalisation." Presented at the Cairns Group Farm Leaders Seminar, November 24, http://cairnsgroup.org/Pages/Unfinished-Business.aspx.

Glauber, J. W., and A. Effland. 2016. "United States Agricultural Policy: Its Evolution and Impact," IFPRI Discussion Paper 01543 (Washington, D.C.: International Food Policy Research Institute).

Glauber, J. W., and D. A. Sumner. 2016. "Cotton Subsidies: The Gifts That Keep on Giving." American Enterprise Institute, June 22, www.aei.org/publication/cotton-subsidies-gifts-that-keep-on-giving/.

Glauber, J. W., and P. Westhoff. 2015. "The 2014 Farm Bill and the WTO." *American Journal of Agricultural Economics* 97, no. 5 (May 9): pp. 1287–97.

Graham, J. P., J. J. Boland, and E. Silbergeld. 2007. "Growth Promoting Antibiotics in Food Animal Production: An Economic Analysis." *Public Health Reports* 122 (January–February), pp. 79–87.

Grow, B., and P. J. Huffstutter. 2014. "U.S. Lawmakers Want to Curb Antibiotic Use on Farms." Reuters (September 16), www.reuters.com/article/us-farm aceuticals-chicken-congress-idUSKBN0HB1YZ20140916.

Harris, G. 2014. "'Superbugs' Kill India's Babies and Pose an Overseas Threat." *New York Times*. December 3.

Headey, D. 2011. "Was the Global Food Price Crisis Really a Crisis? Simulations versus Self-Reporting," Discussion Paper 01087 (Washington, D.C.: International Food Policy Research Institute).

———. 2014. "Food Prices and Poverty Reduction in the Long Run," Discussion Paper 01331 (Washington, D.C.: International Food Policy Research Institute).

Hendrix, C., and B. Kotschwar. 2016. "Agriculture," in *Assessing the Trans-Pacific Partnership: Volume 1: Market Access and Sectoral Issues*, PIIE Briefing (Washington, D.C.: Peterson Institute for International Economics), pp. 41–59.

Hershaw, E. 2016. "When the Dust Settles." *Texas Monthly* (September), www.texasmonthly.com/articles/when-the-dust-settles/.

Hollis, A., and Z. Ahmed. 2013. "Preserving Antibiotics, Rationally." *New England Journal of Medicine* 369 (December 26), pp. 2474–76.

Iceland, C. 1994. "European Union: Oilseeds," in *Reciprocity and Retaliation in U.S. Trade Policy,* edited by T. O. Bayard and K. A. Elliott (Washington, D.C.: Institute for International Economics), pp. 209–32.

Ifft, J., and others. 2012. "Potential Farm-Level Effects of Eliminating Direct Payments," EIB-103 (Washington, D.C.: USDA, Economic Research Service, November).

International Energy Agency (IEA). 2011. *Technology Roadmap: Biofuels for Transport.* Paris.

International Fund for Agricultural Development (IFAD). 2010. *Rural Poverty Report 2011.* Rome.

———. 2016. *Rural Development Report 2016: Fostering Inclusive Rural Transformation.* Rome.

Intergovernmental Panel on Climate Change (IPCC). 2014a. "Summary for Policymakers," in *Climate Change 2014, Mitigation of Climate Change. Contribution of Working Group III to the Fifth Assessment Report of the Intergovernmental Panel on Climate Change,* edited by O. Edenhofer and others (Cambridge University Press), pp. 1–30.

———. 2014b. "Transport," in *Climate Change 2014,* pp. 599–670.

———. 2014c. "Agriculture, Forestry, and Other Land Use," in *Climate Change 2014,* pp. 811–922.

Irwin, S. 2014. "Recent Trends in the Profitability of Biodiesel Production." *Farmdoc Daily* 4, no. 51 (March 19). Department of Agricultural and Consumer Economics, University of Illinois at Urbana-Champaign.

Irwin, S., and D. Good. 2016. "The EPA's Proposed 2017 RFS Standards: Is a Push Still a Push?" *Farmdoc Daily* 6, no. 100 (May 26). Department of Agricultural and Consumer Economics, University of Illinois at Urbana-Champaign.

Ivanic, M., and W. Martin. 2008. "Implications of Higher Global Food Prices for Poverty in Low-Income Countries." *Agricultural Economics* 39, no. 1 (November), pp. 405–16.

———. 2014. "Short- and Long-Run Impacts of Food Price Changes on Poverty," Policy Research Working Paper 701 1 (World Bank).

Jacoby, H. G. 2013. "Food Prices, Wages, and Welfare in Rural India," Policy Research Working Paper 6412 (World Bank).

Krans, B. 2014. "Politics Stall Antibiotics Ban in Congress." *Healthline.* June 22, www.healthline.com/health/antibiotics/politics-pork-and-poultry-why-legislation-has-not-passed.

Krauss, C. 2014. "Dual Turning Point for Biofuels." *New York Times.* April 14.

Kripke, G. 2013. "Digging into the Numbers of the Food Aid Reform Vote in Congress." The Politics of Poverty blog. Oxfam America. June 26, http://

politicsofpoverty.oxfamamerica.org/2013/06/digging-into-the-numbers-of-the-food-aid-reform-vote-in-congress/.

Laborde, D. 2011. *Assessing the Land Use Change Consequences of European Biofuel Policies* (Washington, D.C.: International Food Policy Research Institute).

Landers, T. F., and others. 2012. "A Review of Antibiotic Use in Food Animals: Perspective, Policy, and Potential." *Public Health Reports* 127, no.1 (January-February), pp. 4–22.

Larson, C. 2015. "China's Lakes of Pig Manure Spawn Antibiotic Resistance: Researchers Begin to Size up a Public Health Threat from Burgeoning Pork Production." *Science* 347, no. 6223 (February 13), p. 704.

Laxminarayan, R., T. Van Boeckel, and A. Teillant. 2015. "The Economic Costs of Withdrawing Antimicrobial Growth Promoters from the Livestock Sector," OECD Food, Agriculture and Fisheries Papers 78 (Paris: OECD Publishing).

Laxminarayan, R., and others. 2013. "Antibiotic Resistance – The Need for Global Solutions." *The Lancet Infectious Diseases* 13, no. 12 (December), pp. 1057–98.

Lentz, Erin C., Simone Passarelli, and Christopher B. Barrett. 2013. "The Timeliness and Cost-Effectiveness of the Local and Regional Procurement of Food Aid." *World Development* 39 (September), pp. 9–18.

Levy, S. 2014. "Reduced Antibiotic Use in Livestock: How Denmark Tackled Resistance." *Environmental Health Perspectives* 122, no. 6 (June), pp. A160–65.

Levy, S. B., and others. 1976. "Changes in Intestinal Flora of Farm Personnel after Introduction of a Tetracycline-Supplemented Feed on a Farm." *New England Journal of Medicine* 295, no. 11 (September 9), pp. 583–88.

Liska, A. J., and others. 2014. "Biofuels from Crop Residue Can Reduce Soil Carbon and Increase CO_2 Emissions." *Nature Climate Change* 4, no. 5 (April 20), pp. 398–401, doi:10.1038/nclimate2187.

Maltosoglou, I., and others. 2010. *Household Level Impacts of Increasing Food Prices in Cambodia* (Rome: Bioenergy and Food Security Project, FAO).

Management Systems International. 2012. *USDA Local and Regional Food Aid Procurement Pilot Project: Independent Evaluation Report.* Washington, D.C.

Marshall, B. M., and S. B. Levy. 2011. "Food Animal and Antimicrobials: Impacts on Human Health." *Clinical Microbiology Reviews* 24, no. 4 (October 1), pp. 718–33.

Mathew, A. G., R. Cissell, and S. Laimthong. 2007. "Antibiotic Resistance in Bacteria Associated with Food Animals: A United States Perspective of Livestock Production." *Foodborne Pathogens and Disease* 4, no 2 (June), pp. 115–33.

McEachran, A. D., and others. 2015. "Antibiotics, Bacteria, and Antibiotic Resistance Genes: Aerial Transport from Cattle Feed Yards via Particulate Matter." *Environmental Health Perspectives* 123, no. 4 (January 29), pp. 337–43, doi:10.1289/ehp.1408555.

McKenna, M. 2014. "The Abstinence Method." *Modern Farmer.* June 17, http://modernfarmer.com/2014/06/abstinence-method/.

———. 2015. "The White House 2016 Budget Includes Big Funding for Antibiotic Resistance." *Wired.* January 31, www.wired.com/2015/01/white-house-budget/#more-1719199.

Mellon, M., C. Benbrook, and K. L. Benbrook. 2001. *Hogging It: Estimate of Antimicrobial Abuse in Livestock* (Cambridge, Mass.: Union of Concerned Scientists).

Mitchell, D. 2008. "A Note on Rising Food Prices," Policy Research Working Paper 4682 (World Bank).

National Food Institute, Technical University of Denmark. 2012. *Data for Action,* 2nd ed. For the Danish Integrated Antimicrobial Resistance Monitoring and Research Programme (June). Copenhagen.

National Research Council (NRC). 1980. *The Effects on Human Health of Subtherapeutic Use of Antimicrobials in Animal Feeds* (Washington, D.C.: National Academy of Sciences).

———. 1999. *The Use of Drugs in Food Animals: Benefits and Risks* (Washington, D.C.: National Academy of Sciences).

Naylor, R. 2012. "Biofuels, Rural Development, and the Changing Nature of Agricultural Demand." Stanford Symposium Series on Global Food Policy and Food Security in the 21st Century. Stanford, Calif.

Naylor, R., and others. 2005. "Losing the Links between Livestock and Land." *Science* 310, no. 5754 (December 9), pp. 1621–22.

Ng, F., and M. Aksoy. 2010. "Net Food Importing Countries: The Impact of Price Increases," in *Food Prices and Rural Poverty,* edited by M. Aksoy and B. Hoekman (Washington, D.C.: World Bank and Centre for Economic Policy Research), pp. 139–64.

Nugent, R., E. Back, and A. Beith. 2010. *The Race against Drug Resistance* (Washington, D.C.: Center for Global Development).

Office of Technology Assessment. 1979. "Drugs in Livestock Feed," NTIS order #PB-298450 (Washington, D.C.), June.

———. 1995. "Impacts of Antibiotic-Resistant Bacteria," OTA-H-629 (Washington, D.C.).

OIE (World Organization for Animal Health). 2007. "OIE List of Antimicrobials of Veterinary Importance." May, www.oie.int/doc/ged/D9840.PDF.

Orden, D. 2005. "Can U.S. Farm Subsidies Be Bought Out?" Conference paper presented at the American Agricultural Economics Association, February, www.researchgate.net/publication/23505973_Can_US_Farm_Subsidies_Be_Bought_Out.

———. 2013. "The Changing Structure of Domestic Support and Its Implications for Trade," Paper commissioned by Canadian Agricultural Trade Policy and Competitiveness Research Network. February.

Orden, D., D. Blandford, and T. Josling, eds. 2011. *WTO Disciplines on Agricultural Support: Seeking a Fair Basis for Trade* (Cambridge University Press).

Orden, D., R. Paarlberg, and T. Roe. 1999. *Policy Reform in American Agriculture: Analysis and Prognosis* (University of Chicago Press).

Organization for Economic Cooperation and Development (OECD). 2008. *Biofuel Support Policies: An Economic Assessment* (Paris: OECD Publishing).

———. 2012. *Agricultural Policy Monitoring and Evaluation 2012* (Paris: OECD Publishing).

———. 2016. *Agricultural Policy Monitoring and Evaluation 2016* (Paris: OECD Publishing).

OECD/Food and Agriculture Organization of the United Nations (OECD-FAO). 2012. *Agricultural Outlook: 2012–2021* (Paris: OECD Publishing).

———. 2013. *Agricultural Outlook Summary: 2013–2022* (Paris: OECD Publishing).

———. 2015. *OECD-FAO Agricultural Outlook 2015* (Paris: OECD Publishing).

Persson, M., S. Henders, and T. Kastner. 2014. "Trading Forests: Quantifying the Contribution of Global Commodity Markets to Emissions from Tropical Deforestation," CGD Working Paper 384 (Washington, D.C.: Center for Global Development).

Pew Charitable Trusts. 2014. "Gaps in FDA's Antibiotics Policy." Issue Brief (November 30), www.pewtrusts.org/en/research-and-analysis/issue-briefs/2014/11/gaps-in-fdas-antibiotics-policy.

Polansek, T. 2014. "Big U.S. School Districts Plan Switch to Antibiotic Free Chicken." Reuters, December 9. www.reuters.com/article/us-antibiotics-chicken-education-idUSKBN0JO00320141210.

President's Council of Advisors on Science and Technology (PCAST). 2014. "Report to the President on Combating Antibiotic Resistance." Washington, D.C.

Renewable Energy Policy Network for the 21st Century (REN21). 2014, 2016. "Renewables Global Status Report." Paris, France.

Renewable Fuels Agency. 2008. "The Gallagher Review of the Indirect Effects of Biofuels Production." Report commissioned by the UK Secretary of State for Transport. East Sussex, U.K., www.unido.org/fileadmin/user_media/UNIDO_Header_Site/Subsites/Green_Industry_Asia_Conference__Maanila_/GC13/Gallagher_Report.pdf.

Review on Antimicrobial Resistance (chaired by Jim O'Neill). 2014. *Antimicrobial Resistance: Tackling a Crisis for the Health and Wealth of Nations* (London: Wellcome Trust and U.K. Department of Health).

———. 2016. *Tackling Drug-Resistant Infections Globally: Final Report and Recommendations* (London, U.K.: Wellcome Trust and U.K. Department of Health).

Robinson, T., and F. Pozzi. 2011. "Mapping Supply and Demand for Animal-Source Foods to 2030," Animal Production and Health Working Paper (Rome: FAO).

Rosegrant, M. W. 2008. *Biofuels and Grain Prices: Impacts and Policy Responses* (Washington, D.C.: International Food Policy Research Institute).

Rushton, J., J. P. Ferreira, and K. D. Stärk. 2014. "Antimicrobial Resistance: The Use of Antimicrobials in the Livestock Sector," OECD Food, Agriculture and Fisheries Papers 68 (Paris: OECD Publishing).

Scharlemann, J. P. W., and W. F. Laurance. 2008. "How Green Are Biofuels?" *Science* 319 (2008), pp. 43–44.

Schneider, M. 2011. "Feeding China's Pigs: Implications for the Environment, China's Smallholder Farmers and Food Security." *Institute for Agriculture and Trade Policy Report* (May). Minneapolis.

Schnepf, R. 2008. "Higher Agricultural Commodity Prices: What Are the Issues?," CRS Report for Congress RL34474 (Washington, D.C.: Congressional Research Service), May 29, updated.

———. 2013. "Agriculture-Based Biofuels: Overview and Emerging Issues," CRS Report for Congress R41282 (Washington, D.C.: Congressional Research Service), May 1.

Schnepf, R., and B. D. Yacobucci. 2013. "Renewable Fuel Standard (RFS): Overview and Issues," CRS Report for Congress R40155 (Washington, D.C.: Congressional Research Service), March 14.

Schoneveld, G. C. 2010. "Potential Land Use Competition from First-Generation Biofuel Expansion in Developing Countries," occasional paper 53 (Bogor, Indonesia: CIFOR).

Searchinger, T., and others. 2008. "Use of U.S. Croplands for Biofuels Increases Greenhouse Gases through Emissions from Land-Use Change." *Science* 319 (2008), pp. 1238–40.

Searchinger, T., and R. Heimlich. 2015. "Avoiding Bioenergy Competition for Food Crops and Land." Creating a Sustainable Food Future, Installment Nine (Washington, D.C.: World Resources Institute).

Seymour, F., and J. Busch. 2016. *Why Forests? Why Now? The Science, Economics, and Politics of Tropical Forests and Climate Change* (Washington, D.C.: Center for Global Development).

Sharpe, C. 2014. "Perdue's Next Frontier: Organic." *Delmarva Now,* May 16.

Slayton, T. 2009. "Rice Crisis Forensics: How Asian Governments Carelessly Set the World Rice Market on Fire," CGD Working Paper 163 (Washington, D.C.: Center for Global Development).

Sotak, K. M., M. D. Tokach, M. Hammer, J. Y. Jacela, S. S. Dritz, R. D. Goodband, J. M. DeRouchey, and J. L. Nelssen. 2010. "A Comparison of Denagard, Denagard/CTC and Pulmotil on Nursery Pig Growth Performance and Economic Return" (Kansas State University, Agricultural Experiment Station and Cooperative Extension Service).

Timilsina, G. R., and A. Shrestha. 2010. "Biofuels: Markets, Targets and Impacts," Policy Research Working Paper 5346 (World Bank).

Timmer, P. C. 2005. "Agriculture and Pro-Poor Growth: An Asian Perspective," CGD Working Paper 63 (Washington, D.C.: Center for Global Development), July.

———. 2014. *Food Security and Scarcity; Why Ending Hunger Is So Hard* (University of Pennsylvania Press).

Trostle, R. 2008. "Global Agricultural Supply and Demand: Factors Contributing to the Recent Increase in Food Commodity Prices," USDA Economic Research Service WRS-0801. (Washington, D.C.).

Tyner, W. 2013. "Biofuels and Food Prices: Separating Wheat from Chaff." *Global Food Security* 2, no. 2 (July), pp. 126–30.

U.S. Department of Agriculture (USDA). 2013. *Changing EU Oilseed Market Impacts Global Trade.* Foreign Agricultural Service, International Agricultural Trade Reports. Washington, D.C., July 26.

U.S. Energy Information Administration (EIA). 2012. *Biofuels Issues and Trends.* Washington, D.C.: U.S. Department of Energy, www.eia.gov/biofuels/issues trends/pdf/bit.pdf.

U.S. Environmental Protection Agency (EPA). 2011. "EPA Issues Notice of Data Availability Concerning Renewable Fuels Produced from Palm Oil under the RFS Program," Regulatory Announcement, EPA-420-F-11-046 (Washington, D.C., December).

U.S. Government Accountability Office (GAO). 2009. "International Food Assistance: Local and Regional Procurement Can Enhance the Efficiency of U.S. Food Aid, but Challenges May Constrain Its Implementation," GAO-09-570 (Washington, D.C.), May.

———. 2011. "International Food Assistance: Funding Development Projects through the Purchase, Shipment, and Sale of U.S. Commodities Is Inefficient and Can Cause Adverse Market Impacts," GAO-22-636 (Washington, D.C.), June.

———. 2015. "International Food Assistance: Cargo Preference Increases Food Aid Shipping Costs, and Benefits Are Unclear," GAO-15-666 (Washington, D.C.), June.

Valdes, C. 2011. "Brazil's Ethanol Industry: Looking Forward," BIO-02 (Washington, D.C.: Economic Research Services, USDA).

Van Boeckel, T. P., and others. 2015. "Global Trends in Antimicrobial Use in Food Animals." PNAS (published online ahead of print, March 19), www .pnas.org/content/early/2015/03/18/1503141112.abstract.

Wald, M. L. 2012. "A Fine for Not Using a Biofuel That Doesn't Exist." *New York Times* (January 9).

Ward, M. J., and others. 2014. "Time Scaled Evolutionary Analysis of the Transmission and Antibiotic Resistance Dynamics of *Staphylococcus aureus* Clonal Complex 398." *Applied and Environmental Microbiology* 80, no. 23 (September 19), pp. 7275–82.

Westhoff, P., and others. 2016. "U.S. Baseline Briefing Book: Projections for Agricultural and Biofuel Markets," FAPRI-MU Report #02-16 (Columbia: University of Missouri, Food and Agricultural Policy Research Institute), March.

Wierup, M. 2001. "The Swedish Experience of the 1986 Year Ban of Antimicrobial Growth Promoters, with Special Reference to Animal Health, Disease Prevention, Productivity, and Usage of Antimicrobials." *Microbial Drug Resistance* 7, issue 2 (Summer), pp. 183–90.

Wilson, D., and M. Dwyer. 2014. "Veterinarians Face Conflicting Loyalties to Animals, Farmers—and Drug Companies." *Farmaceuticals* (September 15), www.reuters.com/article/farmaceuticals-vets-idUSL1N0U60Y220141223.

World Bank. 2007. *World Development Report 2008: Agriculture for Development.*

World Health Organization (WHO). 2003. *Impacts of Antimicrobial Growth Promoter Termination in Denmark.* Foulum, Denmark.

———. 2012a. "Critically Important Antimicrobials for Human Medicine: 3rd Revision 2011." (Geneva: WHO Advisory Group on Integrated Surveillance of Antimicrobial Resistance), http://apps.who.int/iris/bitstream/10665/77376/1/9789241504485_eng.pdf.

———. 2012b. *The Evolving Threat of Antimicrobial Resistance: Options for Action* (Geneva).

———. 2014. *Antimicrobial Resistance Global Report on Surveillance* (Geneva).

World Trade Organization, International Trade Center, and United Nations Conference on Trade and Development (WTO/ITC/UNCTAD). 2014. "World Tariff Profiles 2014," (Geneva).

Wright, B. 2014. "Global Biofuels: Key to the Puzzle of Grain Market Behavior." *Journal of Economic Perspectives* 28, no. 1 (Winter), pp. 73–98.

Yacobucci, B. D. 2012. "Biofuels Incentives: A Summary of Federal Programs," CRS Report for Congress R40110 (Washington, D.C.: Congressional Research Service), January 11.

Yacobucci, B. D., and K. Bracmort. 2010. "Calculation of Lifecycle Greenhouse Gas Emissions for the Renewable Fuel Standard (RFS)," CRS Report for Congress R40460 (Washington, D.C.: Congressional Research Service).

Yacobucci, B. D., and R. Schnepf. 2007. "Selected Issues Related to an Expansion of the Renewable Fuel Standard (RFS)," CRS Report for Congress RL34265 (Washington, D.C.: Congressional Research Service).

Zhu, Y.-G., and others. 2013." Diverse and Abundant Antibiotic Resistance Genes in Chinese Swine Farms." *PNAS* 110 no. 9 (February 26): 3435–40.

Zulauf, C. 2013. "Farm Policy Background: Income of U.S. Farm vs. Nonfarm Population." *Farmdoc Daily* (July). Department of Agricultural and Consumer Economics, University of Illinois at Urbana-Champaign, http://farmdocdaily.illinois.edu/2013/07/Farm-Policy-Income-Farm-Nonfarm.html.

———. 2016. "Why Crop Insurance Has Become an Issue." *Farmdoc Daily* 6, no.

76 (April 20). Department of Agricultural and Consumer Economics, University of Illinois at Urbana-Champaign.

Zulauf, C., and D. Orden. 2015. "US Crop Insurance since 1996." *Farmdoc Daily* 5, no. 129 (July 16). Department of Agricultural and Consumer Economics, University of Illinois at Urbana-Champaign.

———. 2016. "Assessing the Political Economy of the U.S. 2014 Farm Bill," *Trade-Related Agricultural Policy Analysis*, edited by D. Orden (Hackensack, N.J.: World Scientific Publishing Co.), pp. 233–70.

Zulauf, C., and others. 2016. "Cottonseed and U.S. Oilseed Farm Program Issues." *Farmdoc Daily* 6, no. 18 (January 28). Illinois: Department of Agricultural and Consumer Economics, University of Illinois at Urbana-Champaign.

Zuraw, L. 2015. "Conversation Begins about How to Collect On-Farm Antibiotic Use Data." *Food Safety News* (October 1). www.foodsafetynews.com/2015/10/conversation-begins-about-how-to-collect-on-farm-antibiotic-use-data/.

INDEX

Center for Global Development

The Center for Global Development works to reduce global poverty and inequality through rigorous research and active engagement with the policy community to make the world a more prosperous, just, and safe place for us all.

The policies and practices of the rich and the powerful—in rich nations, as well as in the emerging powers, international institutions, and global corporations—have significant impacts on the world's poor people. We aim to improve these policies and practices through research and policy engagement to expand opportunities, reduce inequalities, and improve lives everywhere. By pairing research with action, CGD goes beyond contributing to knowledge about development. We conceive of and encourage discussion about practical policy innovations in areas such as trade, aid, health, education, climate change, labor mobility, private investment, access to finance, and global governance to foster shared prosperity in an increasingly interdependent world.

As a nimble, independent, nonpartisan, and nonprofit think tank, we leverage modest resources to combine world-class scholarly research with policy analysis and innovative outreach and communications to turn ideas into action.